W9-CFG-181

THE PHRASE-DROPPER'S HANDBOOK

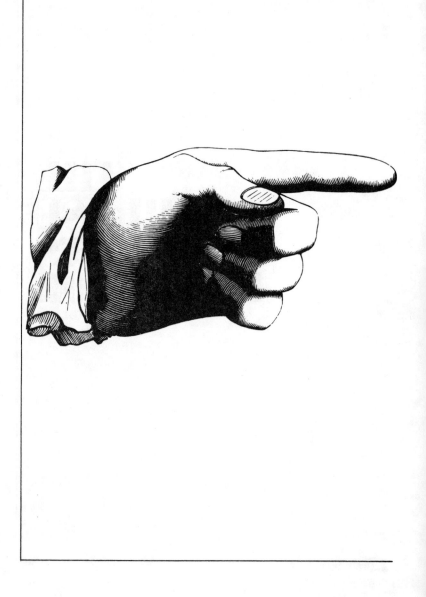

THE PHRASE-DROPPER'S HANDBOOK

John T. Beaudouin
and Everett Mattlin

243 (or maybe it's 312)
field-tested ways to get in,
get out, or get on top
of any conversation.
A convenient guide for the
modestly well-informed.
A manual for appearing
to be educated, sophisticated,
or merely interesting
as you are coping with
conversational overkill,
monologue, or monopoly.

Doubleday & Company, Inc.
Garden City, New York
1976

ISBN 0-385-05519-6
Library of Congress
Catalog Card Number 75–38161
Copyright © 1976 by
Richard F. Dempewolff
and Benjamin R. Hefter, trustees
for Lisa K. Beaudouin, Stephanie B. Piper,
John C. Beaudouin and Mark T. Beaudouin
Printed in the
United States of America
First Edition

In memory of a great editor,
Lee Barker

ACKNOWLEDMENTS

The authors acknowledge with warm thanks the help of the following persons who contributed to this book, some of them without realizing it:

LeBaron R. Barker, Linn Carl, Arthur and Georgina Coleridge, Tess and Louis D'Alpuget, Ursula Dulberg, Oscar Dystel, Joseph W. Hotchkiss, Rosaria and Anatol Konstantin, Warren Lynch, Ken McCormick, Patricia L. Moore, Barbara Patocka, Françoise Pitt-Rivers, Jack Pollard, Jerome Priest, Noel Regney, Stewart Richardson, Ruth Leder Shapiro, Elaine Strainchamps, Leon Tec, M.D., Helen McGrath Tingley, Irving Wisch, Sam Vaughan, and—especially—Maria Beaudouin.

CONTENTS

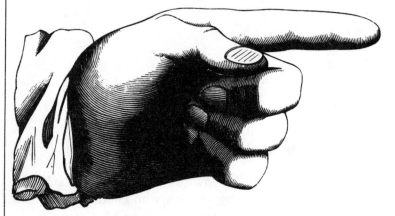

1
INTRODUCTION

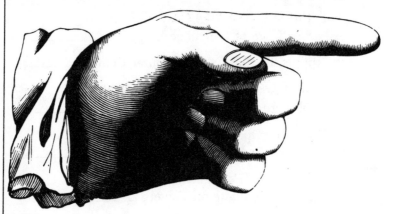

You are standing in a corner of a crowded room, cigarette in one hand, scotch in the other, and nothing in your head to say. A bearded man in a tweed suit with a tweed bow tie and one of those craggy Scandinavian pipes is holding forth, pontificating on the problems of Blight in Our Cities. No one seems able to break his monologue. A few timid questions only stoke his control.

He may be a necktie salesman but he sure knows the jargon. He must have read a book. You, unfortunately, have not—except this one, which is fortunate. For when he mentions something about the new role of the computer in city planning your opportunity has arrived.

"Of course it's not the first time," you put in. "You'll remember that Baron Haussmann had the help of the mathematician Jean Charles Alphand in planning Paris." Keep it casual. "The boulevards were deliberately made a certain width to prevent the building of revolutionary barricades."

No, he doesn't remember—and he is stopped, derailed.

Does this seem like a Walter Mitty fantasy? The situation is real enough. Experts abound. Everyone is full of facts—or opinions—absorbed from fat newspapers, book clubs, TV news, *Time, Newsweek,* the *New York Review,* or precocious children. We are forever surrounded by those who seem to know more than we do.

Well, for those who don't know a way in or out of a conversation, we have written this survival manual. Think of it as a lazy person's guide to coping with conversational overkill. The book will supply you with a manageable catalogue of words, phrases, facts, and quotations, along with simple instructions and technique so that you can hold your own, no matter what the topic. All you need is the book, a modicum of memory, and a pinch of pure gall.

Sure, you *could* read more, go back to school, become educated. But, first, it might not work. Second, you could be set down as a bore. What you need is not true knowledge but the phrase, the bit, the killing fragment.

Next, why do all the work? We've done it for you.

Our motives are innocuous, nearly innocent. They are: to allow you to keep up with the sophisticates, to put down the phonies, to put in with scholars, and to get out alive.

And there may be other advantages to the development of these skills—you may boggle a boss, snow a client, or convince a reluctant lover. But mostly the book is meant as a guide to the game, a game of tongue-in-cheek badinage and verbal bluffery.

Once you have mastered this little primer you will add skills of your own. You can't know it all but you *can* learn to fake it.

All fraud is frightening at first but familiarity will breed content.

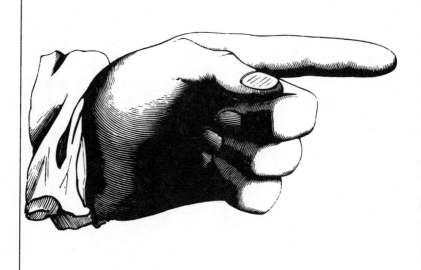

2
ERSATZ ERUDITION:
The Ten Rules

Like any art, conversational counterpoint has its code. The general principles have been handed down —orally, of course, until now—by the masters. In what follows, you will find a modern manual. There are comments on both *content* and *delivery*.

☞ **I. Be dogmatic**

This, like our other instructions, may be disturbing at first. We are all trained in modesty. One must never appear to be a know-it-all. But when pretending to a knowledge you do not have, you must sound totally sure.

If you mispronounce a French word, do it in such a way that the other person will wonder if *he* has been saying it incorrectly all these years. If you combine dogmatic mispronunciation with bold assertions of fact, you are in still stronger shape. Declare that "the St. Emilion '69s shipped poorly" and make it sound like revealed truth. There are not four men on earth able to contradict that line properly delivered.

Flat declarative sentences are the most effective anyhow. Don't say, "If the Catholic vote comes through and Joe Fields does his job with the union locals, Schroeder has a good chance of winning." Do say, emphatically, "Schroeder will take it by 4,700 votes."

What if Schroeder doesn't take it by 4,700 votes? Or doesn't take it at all? No matter. That comes later, days or months after the conversation, and few people will remember. What they will remember is that you are someone who knows politics. The dogmatist beats the pussycat every time.

☞ **II. Spotlight the obscure**

Obviously, avoid the obvious. Know the little-known. Everyone knows that Napoleon blew his cool and his empire at Waterloo. Almost nobody knows that Napoleon may well have lost the day's battle because his hemorrhoids—and an old kidney complaint—slowed him down that morning. The fact must be obscure but arresting.

Everyone is always offering opinions, or arguments, about which Chinese restaurant is the best in town. Mention a restaurant that serves North Korean food and you have put yourself above most competition. When you are ready for the next level, propose the restaurant that serves the *best* North Korean food —and now you're talking.

If the President's Cabinet is under discussion, refer to an undersecretary in the Treasury Department who knows the international monetary problem and who really does all the work. (Or better, an Assistant Secretary of the Interior who knows more about floating rates than all those clods in Treasury. There just might be somebody around who knows that the Treasury undersecretary you have in mind is a statistical illiterate. Nobody knows anybody in Interior.)

Others are comparing Bermuda, Jamaica, and Nassau? Talk about the unblemished purity of Tortola or Virgin Gorda. When the Met's latest production of *La Forza del Destino* is mentioned, endorse last year's staging of Bizet's *The Pearl Fishers*—at Spoleto.

On Elizabeth Taylor's abilities as an actress, comment that she would be just right for Kitty Warren (a character in Shaw's *Mrs. Warren's Profession*). If Hugh Hefner's name or, worse, his "philosophy" comes up, say that "he's just the poor man's Cagliostro" (cal-yo'stro). About a new book by Joyce Carol Oates (you need something new every season), suggest that characterizations of women were better handled by Sarah Orne Jewett.

Two obscure references at once constitute a jab and knockout punch. There seem to be groups who can't avoid talk of Mrs. Onassis. Try: "Jacqueline's style is much more Anne of Cleves than Maria Theresa," which brings most such conversations to a standstill—and should.

The scandalous behavior of some notorious character—say Gabriele D'Annunzio, the Italian writer-patriot—has been dissected in a new book, and someone who has read it is holding forth. Your line is: "Morally speaking, he was by the Marquis de Sade out of Ninon de Lenclos." Thus, in one line, you have stopped traffic in several directions. Of course, a person can overreach. We heard one man's response to a conversation about Jack Nicklaus' failure to win the U. S. Open. He said: "His quiet desperation on the fifteenth was like Saladin's after the fall of Acre."

A corollary to the obscurity principle is: don't be *too* obscure. Assume that your listeners have the usual spotty liberal arts education and try to get them to recognize, *dimly*, what you are talking about. For a time, words like "synergistic" or "symbiotic" were useful but they have been big in business for the last seven-and-a-half years and thus are Out.* But a Latinism like *vade mecum* or referring to *The Castle of Otranto* or the Battle of Lepanto or the Hanseatic League or the acting of Mrs. Siddons—all these are vaguely, nicely, troublingly familiar. Ideally, your mark is most disturbed when he can't quite remember who or what they are, and is too embarrassed to ask.

☞ III. Call upon the past

You are too busy and it is too exhausting to keep up with all that's going on. Besides, everyone reads the

* Study the precise dogmatism of this sentence itself.

same stuff. Turn to the past, therefore, where all is murky and more usefully intimidating.

Someone praises the current Wagnerian soprano's Brünnhilde; you say that Flagstad's was superior— which is probably true anyhow. The Administration's efforts to centralize power in the White House come up every term. Plug in with: "They've got the greatest concentration of power in that basement since Andy Jackson."

"Not since" is standard. "Not since the fourth Lincoln-Douglas debate has there been such a lucid clarification of state's rights." (Note that *"fourth"*; there were seven of them, dummy.) And the rhetorical grandeur of "not since" sets you apart from the crowd before you even complete the sentence:

- "Not since the fall of the Second Temple has there been such a debacle."
- "Not since the Edict of Nantes has there been such an advance in religious freedom."
- "Not since the Gadsden Purchase have we seen such a flagrant disregard of the public interest."
- "Not since Savonarola has . . ."

You can "not since" endlessly. Yes, there are problems. You can't use the Edict of Nantes unless you know that it refers to religious freedom. But if you learn one or two of them, just a little background, even at the risk of really knowing something, you'll find use for "Not since the Missouri Compromise" or "the Council of Trent" or "the Oath of the Tennis Court" or "the Battle of Crécy" and so on.

The historical approach is not only a necessity in some cases, it is safer than other solutions. The further back in time you go the safer you are. The younger the person you are dealing with the better (since the young seem to make it a practice to ignore or blank out history). Do be careful. When Picasso is the topic,

don't bring in Tiepolo if there is any chance that the
curator of the National Gallery is around.

But call upon the past. It is obscure. That's why
we like it.

☞ IV. Specialize

Till one corner of a field and you will appear brilliant without enormous effort.

Make it easy on yourself. Don't try to fake your
way in literature by choosing Faulkner. He wrote too
much and what he wrote is difficult. Find one who is
both obscure and relatively unproductive. Nathanael
West was good for a time, but he has been redis-
covered. Choose someone like Thomas Love Peacock.
His major work, *Nightmare Abbey*, is only 120 pages
long.

In politics, pick Polk or the first Earl of Shaftes-
bury (and pronounce it abbreviated, as "Shafts'bree").
In psychology, take a shadowy figure like Ferenczi or
one chapter of Freud. The one on penis envy does
nicely these days, ringing in psychology, fashion,
women's lib, art, tennis, etc.

For philosophy, try Hume, although that's asking a
great deal; Jainism for religion; and in architecture, nix
Gothic but try Manueline.

Of course, all this is cheating a bit on our rules, for
by doing this you will actually know something. What
preserves the challenge, however, is a *minute* authority, a miniature scholarship.

☞ V. When possible, say it in another language

There are enough obscure English words to intimidate most people, and we'll master a quiverful later.
Nevertheless, a smattering, a muttering, of French,
German, or Latin helps, even if *what* you say provides
no evidence of intelligence. You have no gift for lan-

guages? Fine. Remember, the trick is not to know but to seem to know. More later.

☞ VI. Authorities

This rule is drawn from the master source of all bluffing, the college term paper. Whether you have something to say or not, have a famous name who agrees with you.

Your options are many. But again, avoid the obvious. You can quote the New York *Times* (corny), statistics from the Census Bureau (better), Freud (overworked), Milton the poet or Milton the accountant in your office, who knows everything there is to know about tax returns. Still, the more awesome the *source* the more effective. The name is the game.

Most times you will paraphrase. But a few quotations must be committed to memory. And again, if you can make it sound vaguely familiar, don't bother giving the source. When your neighbor tells you his teen-ager has been calling him a tool of the multi-nationals, murmur, "How sharper than a serpent's tooth . . ." Let him grope for the rest of the quote and its author.

Make up the quote? There's a school that thinks this is dangerous. Sometimes it is the only way out. If a rap on modern educational theory has left you desperate for something to say, or a way to get away, break in with a fabrication: "As Lucretius said, the child without discipline grows into the man without will."

This may require a little talent. In any case, make up the quote as though *you* have the right to be authoritative. Woody Allen, for example, pauses, then intones, "I sometimes think all life is a footnote to Faust." It is especially effective to make up statistics, as needed: "Recent studies show that Nostradamus was wrong 73 per cent of the time."

☞ **VII. Use words in unfamiliar contexts**

At intermission, everyone tries to say something bright about the play and its performers. If you say, "The second act is biodegradable," the sheer lunacy of the comment should turn things your way or at least give you a chance to get to the men's room. Or, "The trouble with the love story, like all love stories, is that it follows a sine curve." Or, "When Joe Papp directs Shakespeare, Heisenberg's uncertainty principle is always operating." Never mind about the meaning: the enigmatic quality of your remarks will set you off as a person of refined perception.

☞ **VIII. On occasion, employ reverse snobbery**

At times this can be dazzlingly effective and sometimes it is the only recourse when the going gets rough. If they are raving about the food at Le Coq d'Or or Rapaccini's Ristorante, look a little bored and offer, "The best dish in town is the corned beef hash at Bickford's Cafeteria." If they are carrying on about Pynchon's or Gaddis' latest unreadable masterpiece, say that you found the new Harold Robbins vastly amusing, more like his earlier serious novels, and yet good trash.

The high scoring here comes from making your audience believe you're so familiar with the highbrow that you can afford to like *shlock*.

☞ **IX. Never punch your lines**

A further word on delivery. What we are engaged in is not a brutal exercise. Use the foil, not the bludgeon. Your shafts of knowledge must be delivered casually, in an offhand, throwaway fashion. What you have just said tripped into your consciousness without effort, the inevitable consequence of breeding, long years of cultural immersion, and a brilliantly retentive mind.

If the other party feels inferior, that's his problem. Punching or emphasizing a line makes your intentions obvious, throws suspicion on your credentials. Give the impression that you speak this way all the time; better still, that everyone else you know does too—except perhaps the person you are talking to at the moment.

·☞ X. Cut your losses quickly

There are those times when you're in too deep, when there's someone too knowledgeable to mess with. This is part of the risk and stimulus of the sport. Don't persist: you're bound to make things worse. Back off before you are whipped—or discovered. Sneeze, see someone across the room, change the subject, utter some high-flown generality, pick at a thread on his sleeve—but get out.

Even in retreat there can be style, as Rommel proved at El Alamein.

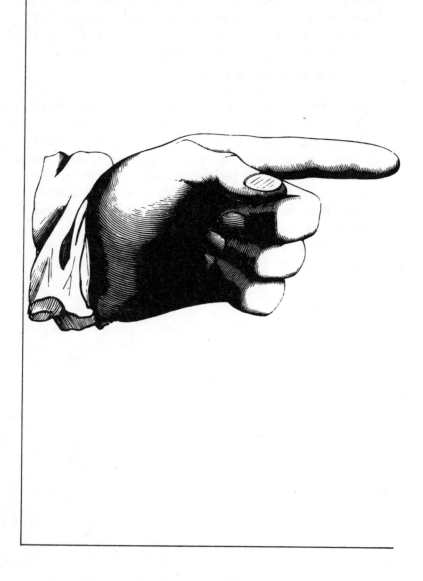

3
A SOUPÇON OF FRANÇAIS IS A MUST

English has no shortage of impressive words, most of them known only to John Simon and William Buckley. But sauce your talk with foreign words or phrases and the banal can be beautiful. Corny or not, you will be labeled a Cultivated Person.

We felt strongly enough about this matter to make it a general principle. The true man (or woman) of the world has the gift of tongues. Speak English alone and you may be alone. Even if your father owns ore boats on Lake Erie and race horses in Lexington, unrelieved English makes you irredeemably small-town, the sort who spends Saturday night with take-out Chinese food and Archie Bunker.

Each foreign language has its own special powers to impress. Still, we must acknowledge that French is the *sine qua non*. (So okay—that's Latin. Don't interrupt.) French is the language of love, diplomacy, couture, society, and the world's most exquisite cuisine. You can't be a fabulous fake without it.

Some people seem to have a natural gift for pronouncing French's liquid *r*'s and nasal *n*'s. A few were reared by French governesses, a few by Berlitz. Some had mums who took them to Biarritz in the summers (we went to Lake George). Intimidating.

But Biarritz or Berlitz, don't panic. We stumbled through French II and we feel secure only with *l'addition, s'il vous plaît, merci, pardonnez-moi,* and *où sont-ils les toilettes?* All you have to do is master a few well-chosen phrases whose pronunciation you can nail down. You start cautiously, with the simplest of interjections, and move on to the heavier stuff as your confidence grows.

☞ **Par exemple,** for starters:

☞**Plus ça change (plew sa shanj),** short for *Plus ça change, plus c'est la même chose* ("The more things change, the more they remain the same"), is a bit of French realism. Using only the first three words flatters those who recognize it into the conspiracy that *we* understand the whole thing. The universality of the comment makes it particularly useful, for human venality, illogicality, and perversity show no signs of abating. Thus, *plus ça change,* delivered with a worldly sigh and left trailing in air, is an all-purpose response to talk of war, peace, political scandal, the breakdown of a second marriage, a traffic jam at a new interchange, or a malfunctioning computer.

☞ **Tant pis (tahn pee),** often a curt and easy way to put a period to a remark you can't handle, means "So much the worse." A professorial type says, "The future of the revolutionary movement is certainly not in this country or in Europe, or even in Africa, but in Latin America." What to say? *"Tant pis"* gives you the last word.

A nice variant is *tant mieux* (tahn meeuh), "So much the better." Almost any change in the world can be handled with *pis* or *mieux,* and if the change *isn't* for the better or the worse, well, then you're back to *plus ça change.*

☞ **Faute de mieux** (fote duh meeuh), "for want of something better," is a bit threadbare, but it is useful to imply you are tired, jaded, have been around so much that most scenes bore you to death. Warning: others may get there first. At a party in a fashionable apartment overlooking New York's East River, one guest casually remarked: "This is such a dreary view compared to the one from my hotel balcony on the Costa 'Smeralda." We smelled trouble. "That was a trip I shan't soon forget. No sooner had we arrived than we were told the Aga Khan had canceled the reception for

foreign dignitaries—and so, *faute de mieux,* we went to
the All-Sardinia Bocce Finals."

☞**Jet set** has almost become standard English so it
may be time to return to one or two older phrases. (A
nice switch is to revive expressions once used beyond
repair—but, it often turns out, not beyond recall.)

☞ **Haut monde (oh mohnd)**, literally, the high or
lofty world, includes all those people who have great
wealth or social position or political clout—or all three.
This takes in most Rockefellers, Duponts, Cabots, Jean
Paul Getty, Henry Kissinger, the Shah of Iran.

They are not to be confused with the *beau monde*
(bo mohnd), "the beautiful people." These are the
names always in "W" and the society columns as they
move from Palm Beach to Marbella (Mar-bay'uh, don't
forget) to backgammon tourneys in Monaco to the
April in Paris Ball in New York: "Babe" Paley, Chessy
Rayner, Serge Obolensky, Princess von Furstenburg,
Mica Ertegun, dress designers and interior designers
(Halston, Bill Blass, Billy Baldwin), fashion magazine
editors who are also rich and social like Diana Vree-
land and Consuelo Crespi, some ex-tennis stars. To add
to the confusion, a certain number of people are au-
thentic members of both the *haut* and *beau mondes.*
The clearest-cut example we can think of is Baron Guy
de Rothschild.

The added virtue of reviving these two phrases is
to make the distinction between them; you can score
on anyone who uses *beau* for *haut,* after you put one or
the other expression into play.

☞ **Manqué (maan-kay)**, unsuccessful, lacking, is a
marvelous little word for one purpose. If you are being
bested in an argument, try: "Helen, you are really a
lawyer *manqué.*" Note the double edge. You are telling
her that she is good at argumentation. You are also slic-

ing the skin delicately with this snippy little Gallicism because she is *not* a lawyer and the suggestion is that she is unfulfilled. Helen has heard the word before but will not be quite certain whether she has been flattered or cut down, while the truth is that you have done both.

☞ **Soi-disant** (swa-dee-zahn'), "so-called" or "self-styled," is a convenient stiletto for puncturing the pretentious. When someone is going on and on about some current fad figure in the arts, you can interject your judgment that Miguel Pinero is only a *"soi-disant* playwright" or Barnet Newman a *"soi-disant* painter" and so on. Your put-down will be so surprisingly abrupt and arbitrary it probably won't even be challenged.

☞ **Revenons à nos moutons** (ruh-vuh-none'   ah noe moo-tawn') translates literally as "Let us come back to our sheep," an expression for which there is not much demand unless you run around with shepherds. Its figurative meaning, "Let's get back to the (main) point," is handier. *Revenons* is best when you have been backed into a corner, for it allows you to change the subject.

You're seated at dinner next to a dowager who is running on about her recent trip to Italy. She is rhapsodizing about her evenings at La Scala and the glories of a particular coloratura soprano. "Yes," you might say, "but her range is limited compared to Galli-Curci's." Remember your role: any time you evoke the past to belittle the present, you have made it tough for your adversary. But suppose the dowager is familiar with great divas of the past and tops you by mentioning yet another great Italian soprano, even further back. If you've used up your capital, change the subject—to one where you're likely to have the upper hand. "True," you say, "but *revenons à nos moutons.* The Italians are a most remarkable people in so many ways. Did you not find on your trip a great deal of praise for Guido Carli? He is probably Europe's most resourceful banker. . . ." Or switch to automobiles and the wonders of the Isotta-Fraschini, or literature and Alberto Moravia, or films or sports or whatever field will allow you to score a quick goal. At least the dowager will retreat to her sinistral partner and leave you to your *cervelle au beurre noir.*

One final, handy phrase for those situations when you either have *no* opinion or can't express clearly what you mean—about a puzzling play, picture, or person: *Ça se sent, ça ne s'explique pas* (Sah suh sahn, sah nuh sex-pleek' pah). It means, "One can feel it, one cannot explain it." Elegant copout, no? And if it conveys the notion of a superb sensitivity that goes beyond mere words . . . well, that's just what you want, isn't it?

18

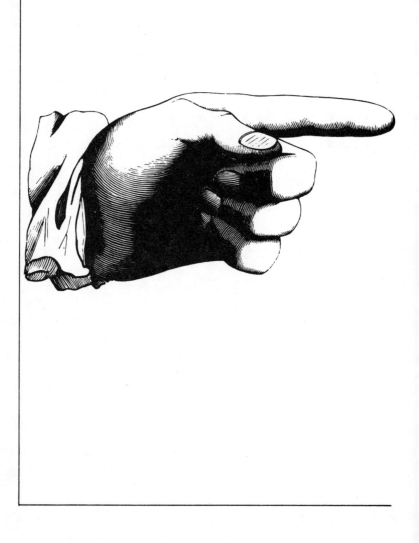

4

EIN BISSCHEN OF DEUTSCH:

It's Hard to Be a Heavy Without It

A chapter on German words must be short. One cannot take too many German words at one time. They are too heavy, thick, lumpy. Most *deutsche* expressions are not for dilettantes.

But that, of course, is precisely their strength. German words intimidate people. Their very *bulk* is awesome. Strange, but almost anything German has this effect. Quoting Hegel, Kant, or Schopenhauer invariably scores more points than Descartes, Rousseau, or Locke. If you listen to Wagner you are obviously a deeper person than one who listens to Verdi. Even a passing reference to a Furtwängler or Schnabel recording hits harder than a disquisition on Toscanini or Monteux.

German language has the same massive proportions as its culture, the same presumed depth, and if you master any of it you assume massive proportions in conversation.

Start with the easier words. You can practice on *gemütlich* (guh-mert'lik), which means agreeable, cheerful, radiating well-being. Say, "How *gemütlich!*" whenever entering a room with a fireplace. It can also be double-edged so your comment can be considered ambiguous or, better still, enigmatic. Sure, *"gemütlich"* verges on a cliché, but it proves you can speak German without stuttering, and such is the forbidding power of anything Germanic that even clichés are strong.

Then go on to the second group:

☞ **Wunderkind** (vun'der-kint), a child prodigy, a real genius of a kid. You use it, of course, to describe your own little Roger, who has just taken up the tuba, but it is especially effective in describing a middle-aged person who has never quite grown up. Oscar Levant, the pianist and professional TV panelist, was called a *Wunderkind* till the day he died.

German is seldom subtle but it offers quite effective depth charges when someone is being overpraised. If everyone is raving about Norman Mailer's latest book, which you have not read and do not intend to, declare, "Norman will always be the querulous *Wunderkind*." (Do not, by the way, confuse this word with the French *enfant terrible*. One Palo Alto lawyer kept calling his neighbor's child an *enfant terrible*, thinking it implied the child was frighteningly precocious, until he found out he was saying the kid was just a bratty little bastard.)

☞ **Angst** (ongst) is a fine word, overused by but redolent of scholarly journals and the *New York Review*, suggesting that the user spends weekends reading paperbacks with titles like *Crosscurrents of Contemporary Epistemology*. All it means is "anxiety," and God knows there's enough opportunity to drag that word through a conversation. You can use it for personal comment—"I don't know if it's my old allergies or an attack of occupational *Angst*"—or to cut up any novelist-poet-artist-performer—"His recent work shows more *Angst* than artistry." A riposte to that kind of dogmatic nonsense is hard to come by.

More positive in its thrust is *Heldenbrust* (held'en-broost), which has come to mean a maiden's heroic-sized bosom. One usually thinks of those Wagnerian Valkyries with the cavernous lungs, but a bit of license is allowed here, permitting the word to refer to a better-than-average bikini stuffer.

☞ **Echt** (ekt), genuine, the real thing. This is rather a funny little word, sounding like an expletive (echt!), and it can be used playfully, as in referring to the noted German playwright's *Mother Courage* as "*echt* Brecht," or combining it with Yiddish and a 180° turn to note that "the Frobishers' furnishings strike me as *echt shlock* [true junk]."

☞ **Kitsch** (kitch), cheap or tawdry. This has long been in vogue, implying that something is so awful it has at best a campy attraction, like hideous Victorian bric-a-brac. (An excellent example was the New York *Times*'s reference to Miami's Fontainebleau Hotel as "the Parthenon of kitsch.")

But such words are popguns compared to the heavy artillery available. The German flotilla offers words freighted with the cargo of Germanic scholarship, of Schlegel and Schleiermacher, of Nietzsche and Treitschke, whose names are unpronounceable and works impenetrable. Commit several of these words to memory and the Maginot Line of the learned dissolves.

☞ **Zeitgeist** (zite'geist), "the spirit of the times." This is a favorite of historians and sociologists, but try it on a more mundane level: "The length of your son's hair is no cause for concern; it's only a reflection of the leftover *Zeitgeist* of the sixties."

☞ **Schadenfreude** (shod'en-froid-uh), a singularly German word, describes the mixture of pleasure and guilt one feels at the misfortune of another. As, "When I heard that Harry got the ax, I must confess I was overwhelmed with *Schadenfreude*—as well as the essential justice of the decision."

☞ **Weltschmerz** (velt'shmairtz) is nice: anguish or pain about the state of the world. Useful when self-directed or in spoken self-analysis. This is what you tell yourself you have when you feel too troubled to do any real work. Or when you are down because, for the eighty-fifth day, the stock market is down. But you can be unsympathetic when others are depressed. "Maybe it's *Weltschmerz* Arthur is suffering from, but more likely it's that he's put on twenty pounds while Marsha has lost ten."

☞   **Weltgemeinschaft** (velt-guh-mine′shoft),   a word with the muscles of a Ruhr miner, means "a world-embracing organization." This ponderous number should be used only as the pompous last word on a weighty subject about which you have no real information. As, "Well, no one knows what the commission's report will bring, but as I see it, the imperative of the moment is for a true *Weltgemeinschaft*." You may add, "A *Weltgemeinschaft* of the public-spirited." Or of the C.I.A., etc.

☞   **Weltanschauung** (velt′on-show-ung) is another word with "world" in it—the Germans are always looking for universals. This one means a total way of looking at and interpreting the world. It's a word without which many literary critics would be speechless. You can put a period to a political discussion with: "It's not in Sadat's *Weltanschauung*." Or, "Kissinger's *Weltanschauung* is a mix of Teddy Roosevelt, Bismarck, and Walt Disney."

☞   **Fingerspitzengefühl** (*fing*-ger-shpitz′en-guh-fewl) is a funny-looking mouthful that means the ability to feel, or sense, through the fingertips—subtle intuition, German style. The *whole* word is great if you can handle it. If not, try the short form, thus: "Sam may not have too many smarts but he's got something just as good: the old *fingerspitz*."

Such words are blockbusters. Use them sparingly. Keep them in reserve for otherwise lost battles.

Since one German word can be devastating, consider the effect of a string of them. A quotation from the most august and revered of all German writers, Goethe, is your opportunity. Commit this one to memory, practice it regularly, and you will move safely among the most threatening of adversaries. We choose it because of its adaptability to almost any conversation. What is under discussion? The fate of the Middle East? The National Football League playoffs? You have only to look wise and intone solemnly, "It is easy for us to be critical after the fact, but remember Goethe: *'Der Mensch denkt, Gott lenkt.'*"

If someone should dare, however timidly, to ask your meaning, patiently translate: "Man proposes, but God disposes." Incontestable. Inscrutable. So is Goethe. So are you.

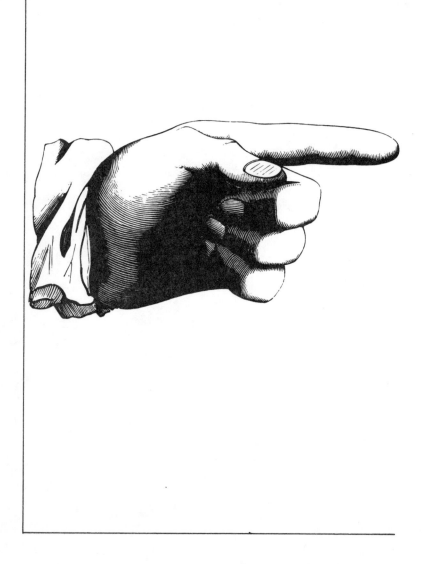

5
YIDDISH:
Talking Softly
but Carrying
a Big Shtick

Just as the upper and older classes take on the talk of youth, hippies, and other minorities whose speech they once scorned as vulgar, so a word of Yiddish dropped here and there is now chic. Even educated, rich, and/or assimilated Jews utter Yiddish phrases from time to time.

The trouble is, for our purposes, that the trend·has gone too far. Every television comedian uses Yiddish, and many words have been naturalized into American slang. One thinks immediately of *chutzpa* (roughly, huts'pah—or, as Leo Rosten puts it, as though you were trying to extricate a fishbone from the roof of your mouth); it means unmitigated nerve or gall.

Then, of course, there's *kibitzer* (kib'it-ser), an onlooker who offers unsolicited comments on a card game or any proceeding; *klutz* (klutts), a chronically clumsy person or bungler; *shtick* (shtik), one's forte, or an act, a performer's piece of business; and, at the next level, *kvetch* (kuh-vetch), *kvetcher*, a verb meaning to complain or one who is a chronic complainer; *yenta* (yen'ta), a female busybody who mixes in others' affairs; also, an abrasive, loud, unmannerly person; *meshuggener* (meh-shoog'in-ah), an irrational or wildly unpredictable person; the *shlemiel* (shle-meel'), who can't do anything right; *shlimazl* (shle-mozz'l), a Joblike character to whom everything bad happens, for whom the short end of the stick is the only end. The waiter who spills a bowl of soup is a *shlemiel*, the man he spills it on is the *shlimazl*.

Also consider *mavin* (may'vin), an expert, a connoisseur, or at least a devotee; *nosh* (nosh), a snack, or to eat a snack, usually with gusto; *shmoos* (shmoose), to gossip or talk at length about nothing important; *nu* (noo?), often used as a question meaning "What's the story?" or as in "So what's new?"; *shmendrick* (shmen' drik), a weak, unreliable person; *momser* (mom'ser), an evil person, a true-blue bastard.

All too familiar, as common as bagels and lox? To some of your acquaintances, perhaps, but certainly not to all. And try using them in an unexpected context: "What Genet is peddling is *shlock* existentialism."

Master a few uncommon Yiddish words. The following, acceptable at this writing, are subject to change without notice. If any one is heard on three talk shows, drop it.

☞ **Shtarker** (shtar'ker); a star, one of real importance. "The trouble with Burt Reynolds is his preoccupation with being a *shtarker.*"

☞ **Kvell** to be full of pride: "And there was this whole roomful of fresh-faced young graduates, their parents *kvelling* in the background . . ."

☞ **Shmatte** (shmot'ta), a rag. "My dear, she says it's a Givenchy, I say it's an original *shmatte.*"

☞ **Megillah** (meh-gil'ah); a rigmarole, a long, boring recital or a long, boring anything. "His inaugural speech was a *megillah* masterpiece."

☞ **Shmeer** to bribe. "O'Connor must have *shmeered* every wardheeler in town to get the nomination." Also, nicely enough, used to denote a *shmeer* of cheese on a bagel. And it also means "the whole package, or deal."

☞ **Mechaieh** (ma-ky'ah), a pleasure, a great joy. "The exquisite control of Baryshnikov and Kirkland in the *pas de deux* was a *mechaieh.*"

☞ **Macher** (mahk'er) is going out and *gonif* has gone. But if you happen to find yourself in a roomful of downstate Illinois folks, say, who don't pick up on a lot of yesterday's Yiddish, you could ring in one or the other. *Macher*, big shot, a man of some power, works like this: "Stevenson may head the Executive Committee in that organization but old Pete is the real *macher.*"

Thief, of course, is the ancient definition for *gonif* (gon'iff) and it still has a thousand uses, in discussions ranging from politics to penitentiaries (not really a range, of late). "My ex-broker is with the most prestigious house on the Street—but in my book he's a *gonif*. Now that I think of it, they're *all* gonifs down there. That's the name of his firm, in fact: 'Shtarker, Shnorrer, and Gonif.' "

Which brings us to *shnorrer* (shnor'er), a parasite, a sponger. "Sam can't save a nickel—his relatives are bleeding him silly. Those who aren't vultures are straight *shnorrers*."

Yentz (pronounced just as it looks), literally means to fornicate, but more casually or generally means to cheat: "Watch out for Larry, he'll *yentz* you any way he can."

Two useful phrases are *Abi gezind* (ah-bee guh-zint') and *Hok mir nit kain tchynik* (Hock meer nit kine chy'nik). The first, "as long as you have your health," is a response to almost any kind of bad news. "My partner just cleaned out our cash and ran off with my wife." The only response: "*Abi gezind.*"

Literally, the second phrase translates as, "Don't beat on my teakettle," but that sounds just like a translation. Instead, it has the force of "Don't bug me" or "Don't pester me with so much talk." Useful in dealing with a nagging spouse, a noisy, irritating child, a creditor, or as an exit line in a conversation.

Of course, any of the above words and phrases used at a bar mitzvah would be wasted. They are effective only in the proper setting—that is, the ostensibly *im*proper setting. They should be spoken at WASP gatherings where their mild shock value will register. What is needed, in other words, is a little *chutzpa* at the Union League.

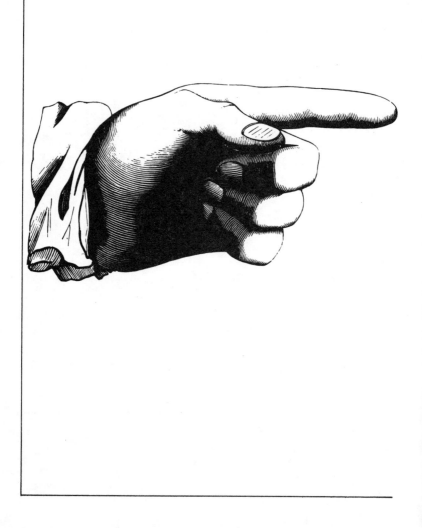

6
LATIN:
Still, You Might Say,
the *Ne Plus Ultra*
of Languages

A *soupçon* of French, *ein bisschen* of German, and a *bissel* of Yiddish, and you are as well prepared as if you knew what you were talking about. You have a little purse of words to spend as needed, to purchase the final say in discussions or to buy your way out of a tough spot.

There *are* other languages, of course, and by all means cultivate scraps as you can. When Marcello Mastroianni was the new international screen idol, there wasn't a model, copy writer, or bartender in New York who didn't yodel *ciao* as a greeting or farewell. *Prego* (You're welcome) is fun, and you might mutter, "Damned *paparazzi* [free-lance, leechlike photographers who bother celebrities]!" when passing a newsstand lined with those scurrilous magazines framing— in more ways than one—Jacqueline Onassis on their covers.

A Russian word or two—try *spasibo* (spah-see′buh) —is a kick. "*Spasibo?* Oh, just the way Russkis say 'thank you.' " *Nye pa̱lozhna* (nee′yeh pol-ozh′nah), meaning "not permitted," is handy for when you've tired of *verboten.* You should also know the Greek word *hubris,* a favorite of intellectuals, like the German *welt* words. "The excessive pride that goeth before a fall" is handily summed up in that one short word and it helps when referring to what happened to Oedipus and Agamemnon and Prometheus and Orestes and Jason and almost any other Greek *macher* you could name.

But if you want to do advanced work, bone up on a few words of Latin. Yes, Latin, the high school horror. Dead, but puissant in death. Say what you will, Latin has power. The speaker isn't merely bright and traveled, someone who's picked up a few phrases, he is *learned,* by God. It all has to do with the glory of the ancients and the language in which they immortalized their wisdom. Latin's dominance as the queen of snob languages is, well, irrefragable.

Now no one expects you to go back and bury yourself in the dust of *amo, amas, amat*. That is not our way. Just adopt a few of the following.

On a very elementary level, for example, one easily uses *ad hoc* (ad hock), something designed "for the case at hand," for a specific situation. Every joiner has served at one time on an *ad hoc* committee, but few know what *ad hoc* really means; they usually assume it has something to do with the committee's importance. The beauty of *ad hoc* is that it can so easily be injected into any conversation. "If a problem crops up on the Mergenthaler contract," you can tell your secretary in a voice loud enough for your boss to hear, "we'll deal with it on an *ad hoc* basis." (If the boss murmurs, "That's the way you deal with everything," start looking for a new job.)

Another ordinary phrase is *De gustibus* (day goose' tee-bus), short for *De gustibus non est disputandum*, "There is no disputing about tastes." When someone extols the superiority of an artist, a book, or a restaurant you've never heard of, shake your head in seeming disbelief and sigh, "*De gustibus . . .*"

Other workaday Latinisms include:

☞ **quid pro quo** (kwid proe kwoe), "one thing in return for another." As, "So I told my wife if she's so hot for Women's Lib and my doing the dishes, fine—*quid pro quo*, she can damn well fix the power mower."

☞ **deo volente** (day'oe voe-len'tay), "God willing," is easy to throw into a sentence, and look, Ma! you're speaking Latin. If someone says Jim Bouton should become manager of the New York Yankees, you can reply, "*Deo volente*, I will not live to see it."

☞ **mirabile dictu** (mi-rab'i-lay dik'too), "wonderful to relate," has the same amiable flexibility. "I told Margaret she didn't know what she was talking about and, *mirabile dictu*, she agreed."

☞ **carpe diem** (kar'pay dee'em), "seize upon—or

enjoy—the day." "How can we be sanguine about the future of a country where the young are suckled on a *carpe diem* philosophy?"

☞ **infra dig** short for *infra dignitatem,* "beneath one's dignity." "To apologize to that person would be strictly *infra dig.*" Or, in the blue denim version, "Sucking up to that pig would be *infra dig,* dig?"

☞ **ne plus ultra** (nay ploos ultra), perfection, the ultimate. "The Savoy, Claridge's, the Connaught—marvelous old hotels, yes, but the Bristol in Paris is the *ne plus ultra.*"

☞ **lapsus linguae** (lap'sis ling'gwee). Convenient to substitute for "lapse" or "slip of the tongue," which it means. "I said his book is stolid? My, my. I thought I'd said 'solid.' Must have been a *lapsus linguae.*" This is tonier than calling it a Freudian slip.

☞ **cum grano salis** (kum grah'no sah'lis). You guessed it, "with a grain of salt." "If Clyde claims he's been shooting in the low 70s, take it *cum grano salis.*" Also, a nice way to drink Margaritas.

☞ **terra incognita** (ter-ra in-cog-neet'a), "an unknown country." "I know Arthur's way past twenty, but I have a feeling the female body is still *terra incognita* to that boy."

After you have a few simple phrases at the ready it is time to master longer and rarer items. As always, you need two or three so general that their application can be almost universal.

Choose from among the following:

☞ **quod licet Jovi non licet bovi** (quoad lye'set Jo'vye nohn lye'set bo'vye), "What is permitted to Jove is not permitted to an ox," or, more freely, "What a god may do, an ox may not." Next time the gang is bitching in the cafeteria over the fact that you have an assigned space in the parking lot and they don't, lay this one on them. Make sure you've finished your lunch first; you may have to get out fast.

☞ **alia jacta est** (al'ee-a jak'ta est), "The die is cast." Short and sweet. The appropriate comment after all three couples have agreed that this time it will be Mexican instead of Chinese food. Or to trade keys to their villas.

☞ **quis custodiet ipsos custodes?** (kwis   cus-toe' dee-et ip'sos cus-to'dace), "Who shall guard the guards themselves?" Work this into the next discussion of police corruption, Pennsylvania Avenue, the F.B.I. director, or, if it's still around, the C.I.A.

☞ **timeo Danaos et dona ferentes** (tim'ee-oe da-nay'-oes et do'na fer-en'tace), "I fear the Greeks even when bearing gifts." Remember this one? The Trojan Horse, wily Ulysses? This is useful for foreign affairs discussions, especially re (Latin) our relations with the Russians and the Chinese. Or the Arabs and Israelis. Greeks, Turks, Kurds, etc.

☞ **de mortuis nil nisi bonum** (day   mor'too-is   nill nee'see boe'num), "Say nothing but good of the dead." Neat way to imply that something good to say would be hard to find. Especially useful in discussing one's family.

As an example of how these might be employed in everyday life, let's look at a situation in which young Roger Devoe, public relations executive, is vying for a new account. The decision will be made by Philmore Hollingswood, Amherst '38, who prides himself on his erudition. He doesn't want just another PR agency; he wants profound and thoughtful discussions of image, positioning, public information, and the role of the ombudsman with a consultant-colleague who has his respect. Roger's rival is Theodore Dempster, another PR man who, as fate would have it, is also Amherst, class of '56.

All three belong to the Midtown Athletic and Sybaritic Club where, the very week Hollingswood is to decide, they chance to meet in the lounge. Knowing of the executive's respect for learning, Ted Dempster tries to dredge up something suitable from the Sunday *Times:*

"I see that a new annotated edition of Leibnitz has just been published by the University of Tübingen Press. I dare say scholars will now pay more attention to the old boy, and Newton's overblown reputation could be clipped a jot or two."

Hollingswood is pleased. "Yes, I saw that in the *TBR* too. And it will be interesting to see if new light is cast on Leibnitz's influence on Spinoza."

Roger writhes. He has not seen the item and has always thought Leibnitz invented optics or something of the sort. And what the hell is the *TBR?* Oh—the *Times Book Review,* okay. He chances all.

"Newton, Spinoza, Leibnitz—all were of an age when truth was of a whole, not fragmented as in our disjointed time." That seems safe enough. He decides to push on. "And each one had the clear vision of the seer, those who stare unflinchingly at universals. We miss such giants today. The world is full of pigmies—except for a business leader or two." Dempster is clearly uncomfortable. Roger moves in for the kill. "But then, *magna est veritas, et praevalebit* [truth is mighty, and will prevail]."

Dempster is speechless. Hollingswood is delighted. Roger has triumphed. The signed contract will be sent to him forthwith.

Our scenario is not as preposterous as it might sound. A surprising scattering of executives dropped a prospective academic career "because of the old meal ticket." And these days, when almost everyone has been to college, there is more respect for a flash of erudition than some years back when self-made dropouts looked askance at bookworms or eggheads.

We bring this up because one can get gratifying

mileage, in memos and letters, from a subtle seeding of Latinisms. They are like asterisks reminding others of one's lifetime credentials. Watch Frobisher take a shot across the bow:

☞ **Q.E.D.** (*quod erat demonstrandum*), "which was to be proved." "Mr. Frobisher claims the shipment will arrive on the 18th. This is impossible, since past invoices indicate a minimum of 5 days shipping time and the 16th is a holiday. Q.E.D."

☞ **C.** is an abbreviation for *circa*, "about" or "around." "George Frobisher's last venture in currency hedging in our foreign operations, c. 1971, will remind us how careful we must be in this area."

☞ **Q.V.** (*quod vide*), "which see," a reference point or precedent. "I think Frobisher will have trouble with Washington on this one, judging by I.C.C. vs. Interstellar Trucking, *q.v.*"

Now Frobisher, hit below the line, begins to take on water. "Frobisher's blunders in his report are almost too numerous to deal with, but I shall take them up *seriatim*" (ser-ee-ay'tim), "serially" or "in sequence."

☞ **sic** (seek), a little flag that indicates the word just used was printed exactly as it was given. If someone has made a mistake, this is the approved way to poke at it. "Frobisher just told the Board he was in favor of a dividend cut irregardless (*sic!*) of its effect on investor confidence."

☞ **D.V.** standing for the *Deo volente* we have already encountered, is the *coup de grâce*. "After the new executive staff takes over, we'll have seen the end of Frobisher, *D.v.*"

Poor Frobisher, drifting out of sight, listing from salvos of Latin. Hope he never sees the memos. (He stopped being "carboned" months ago.) All those funny words and initials would only add to his discomfort. But then, he had his days as a regnant V.P., and, as the ancients said, *sic transit gloria mundi*.

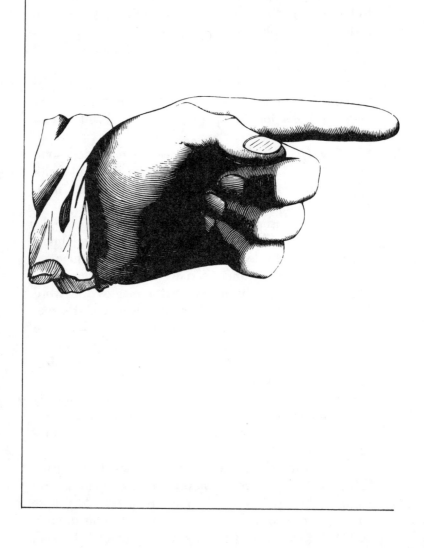

7

"INPUTS, OUTPUTS":
A Computer
Compote

The computer is a faceless monster, possibly benign. Its expanding importance in our lives is obvious, yet most of us with liberal educations know almost nothing about these awesome machines. This makes it ideal for the conversational con man, for a little information can go a long way. Computerese *in extenso* is a drag, but a smidgen of authoritative technological talk has the clout of Darwin dilating on monkeys.

Jousting with an electronics engineer, of course, could be a disaster, though even here we will be brash enough to suggest certain gambits. But the way to use the jargon is in non-computer fields, and it can be used with dramatic results. Suppose a group is discussing the latest crisis on Capitol Hill. You shake your head and intone, "The input is not there yet for Congress to make a turnaround." Impressive—for you have made a *technological sound*. No one can quarrel with a computer.

Now, however, you must become familiar with other words. The lesson will be short.

Hardware and *software* are not, in this field, nuts and bolts or cashmere sweaters. Although overused lately, using them in a non-computer sense can jolt anyone you are talking with into a panicky rearrangement of associations, giving you the upper hand for the few seconds it takes to seize the initiative.

Hardware is indeed the hard, physical computer—all the machinery, including the punch cards, magnetic tape, or magnetic discs that feed in the data, or *input*. Software is the "program," the instructions for the computer, what you tell the hardware to do. What issues forth is called *output*. The instructions are carried out in a *central processing unit* or *CPU*. (Another name for the CPU is *mainframe*.)

When a business friend says his inventory control

is now being computerized, you can ask, "Where's the CPU?" Or when local school problems are being debated over dinner, you pop up with, "It's not the hardware I'm concerned about"—meaning sufficient schools and gyms and blackboards—"but the software," implying that the faculty and the Board of Education are a bunch of dolts. In this application, "software" can refer to almost any management.

A few more useful terms. Two are familiar because they are much used in other fields as well: *interface*, referring to a unit that has to be plugged into another component. A readily transferable word, as in, "I refuse to talk to that damn mechanic any more. Mabel is my interface—we're plug-to-plug compatible." The other term is *turnaround*. This is simply the time it takes to process the input and get the output back to a client. Again, one can use such terms liberally: "You're waiting for a memo on it? Well, tell Charley to send me those figures, and he can have an hour's turnaround."

☞ **Terminal.** This is a device that readies the input data (like that?) for transmission to a CPU. Or, on the other end, it can convert output into something we can read and understand. The telephone instrument is really a terminal for voice communication. Try, "It's no good asking Hawkins. Whenever he explains anything, you need a terminal to convert it into English."

☞ **Virtual storage.** All sorts of data—"previous input and output material"—has to be stored, to be used as needed for new projects. Virtual storage is the system that juggles all this material, partly on tapes and discs, partly still in the CPU itself, to achieve this end. So, you say, in the right company, "When it comes to who won which quarrel ten years ago, and what I said, my wife has a virtual storage system that is frightening."

With.this modicum of terminology, you could at least hold your own with other laymen who have a smattering of ignorance. When you come across someone who *really* knows something about computers—a real live programmer, say—you have a problem.

We would retreat at that point were it not for the buttressing of a friend, Jerry Priest, hardheaded boss of his own software company. Jerry says that the field is relatively so new, so much in flux, that no one feels too secure. If you simply strike at the insecurity, you can be agreeably surprised. His ploys:

First, if you are befuddled by an expert's assertions—on the impact of computers on city planning or on executive compensation or whatever—never confess it. Bring the conversation back to your plane by saying, "What you say is very interesting, but it would be helpful to the others here if you put your thesis in laymen's terms." Chances are excellent that he can't.

Alternatively, pretend you understand it all, but challenge: "What you say is well and good, but what about the trade-offs?"—i.e., options—is another variant that may throw him. Or, "From what I hear, the economics will kill the program." If you want to sound even more authoritative, "It's conceded there's a price performance feasibility problem."

Failing all else, Jerry advises one sentence for desperate situations. "There are definite possibilities in what you suggest, but I don't see anyone solving the deflection problem—and when they do there's the materials challenge left to consider."

Never mind knowing what it all means. Use it as needed and be grateful.

A friend at the Honeywell Company devised a devilish tool so that anyone who can count to ten can compose up to—say the Honeywell computers—40,000 well-balanced and most impressive sentences that are sheer gobbledygook. (See Table A.)

To use it, a person thinks of a four-digit number. Any four-digit number will do—1492, for instance. Now, he reads phrase 1 off the first group—which they call, in computer land, Module A—phrase 4 off Module B, phrase 9 off Module C, and phrase 2 off Module D. Thus, he comes up with:

"In particular, initiation of critical subsystem development effects a significant implementation of the anticipated fourth-generation equipment."

You can spin off a whole conversation, even a report, this way, simply by adding more four-digit sentences. The modules can be arranged in other sequences: DACB, BACD—it will still work. "In these advanced configurations," warns the Honeywell man dryly, "some additional commas may be required."

TABLE A

MODULE A	MODULE B
1. In particular,	1. a large portion of the interface coordination communication
2. On the other hand,	2. a constant flow of effective information
3. However,	3. the characterization of specific criteria
4. Similarly,	4. initiation of critical subsystem development
5. As a resultant implication,	5. the fully integrated test program
6. In this regard,	6. the produce configuration baseline
7. Based on integral subsystem considerations,	7. any associated supporting element
8. For example,	8. the incorporation of additional mission constraints
9. Thus,	9. the independent functional principle
10. In respect to specific goals,	10. a primary interrelation between system and/or subsystem technologies

MODULE C

1. must utilize and be functionally interwoven with
2. maximizes the probability of project success and minimizes the cost and time required for
3. adds explicit performance limits to
4. necessitates that urgent consideration be applied to
5. requires considerable systems analysis and trade-off studies to arrive at
6. is further compounded when taking into account
7. presents extremely interesting challenges to
8. recognizes the importance of other systems and the necessity for
9. effects a significant implementation of
10. adds overriding performance constraints to

MODULE D

1. the sophisticated hardware.
2. the anticipated fourth-generation equipment.
3. the subsystem compatibility testing.
4. the structural design, based on system engineering concepts.
5. the preliminary qualification limit.
6. the evolution of specifications over a given time period.
7. the philosophy of commonality and standardization.
8. the greater fight-worthiness concept.
9. any discrete configuration mode.
10. the total system rationale.

8

DON'T JUST STAND THERE, SAY SOMETHING OBSCURE:
On Culture in General

Culture has long since ceased to be un-American. To be sure, intellectuals like to think their subjects are more likely to be discussed at a cocktail party in Manhattan (N.Y.) than at one in Manhattan (Kan.), but they're wrong. Thanks to the media and the education explosion, Pop Kulch has gone national, and you have to be prepared for some pretty heavy stuff anywhere.

Every art form has its special language, naturally, but there are techniques that can be used for all. In our first chapter we suggested that you call upon the past. This is particularly helpful in cultural matters, because if everyone is seeing the same foreign films and reading the same *Time* or *Times* book reviews, your only chance is to hark back to earlier, unfamiliar periods.

• "Bertolucci's evocation of mood is skillful, but feeble, really, compared to *The Cabinet of Dr. Caligari.*"

• "Nureyev is striking but so much more self-conscious than Nijinsky."

• "Granted, Voznesenski's poetry has some power, but have you reread Lermontov lately?"

• "Jan Kott's evaluation of *Othello* entirely misses the point. Read Colley Cibber."

Such comparisons may not make sense, but time is on your side. Fewer and fewer people know whether Laurette Taylor ever played Hedda Gabler or Toscanini recorded the Spring Symphony or Rosa Ponselle sang *Carmen*. The further back your references, the safer your ground.

You are also safest when you are most obscure. In literature, always ignore an author's major works and praise the least-read one—Melville's *Omoo*, for example, or Shakespeare's *Titus Andronicus*. Or talk about Joyce's play, *Exiles*, instead of his novels; or Thomas Hardy's poetry; or Bernard Shaw's music criticism.

The obscurity *shtick* is also useful when attending concerts, plays, operas, or gallery openings. Overblown pronouncements, even if sheer nonsense, will also work. Here, conversation is a special trial. Everyone tries to come up with "significant" comments about the work. Try these—and remember to speak in italics:

• (Theater): "The lighting in the second act is *much* too bright for the mood."

• (Piano recital): "His articulation of the arpeggios was crystalline." Or, "His reading is icily percussive, *totally* free of romantic involvement."

• (Gallery opening): "Rauschenberg really is showing at a disadvantage in that gallery. Their hanging is simply *un*believable."

• (Theater): "The play doesn't achieve a true catharsis—it simply orchestrates our *tensions*."

• (Violin recital): "Remarkable violinistic *machismo*." Or, the tool ploy, comment on the instrument: "The Guarnerius del Gesù he's using tonight makes a *real* difference, don't you think?"

• (Opera): "Those sets are getting tacky—someone *must* give the Met a new production of *Tristan*."

• (Concert): "Where could you hear a more controlled and yet *freer* sense of rubato?" Or, "His touch never failed him—even at the most perilous *presto*."

If you want to risk a little, choose one of the lesser-known authors or artists and become completely familiar with that individual's work—preferably one whose output is limited. Among contemporary novelists, for example, you might choose Walker Percy, Jerzy Kosinski, William Gaddis, Harvey Swados, or James Purdy.

A French or German novelist is even better, of course, and we used to score occasionally with the

Brazilian, Machado de Assis (ma-shah'do dih ah-seez').

Let's say you've read two or three of the novels—in translation, of course—of Nathalie Sarraute (Sahr-oat). When the discussion turns to Updike or Mailer or Roth, you say, "Yes, but the same ironic juxtaposition of personal and social values is handled more skillfully by Sarraute." If someone has the innocence—and courage—to ask, "Who is he?" you strike again. Patiently, you explain that the "he" is a "she" and plunge into your Sarraute spiel, which gives you control of the conversation, and you can lead it out of dangerous waters.

An improved strategy is to employ words that have universal application to any art form but are vague in definition. They sound impressive and a few, even used carelessly, will cow others nicely. Consider:

☞ **existential.** No matter that this word has been part of intellectual patois ever since Sartre sipped his first absinthe. It is still a word with some power, for few people know quite what it means. And it can be programmed at will to any field. Thus: "That book/play/painting/opera/film redefines the existential experience of the neurotic personality."

surreal. A similar curve to throw at the glib. Yes, it means "beyond the real" somehow, but that leaves a lot of leeway. So just use it without inhibition, especially when called upon for comment on any work you don't understand at all. "Yes, I saw the last Buñuel film. It had a surreal quality reminiscent of Cocteau, wouldn't you say?" With a few nouns changed, such a sentence will work well in an analysis of a shrimp omelette made by last weekend's hostess.

☞ **Jungian.** "Freudian" is too tired, but "Jungian" suggests deeper knowledge. Jung wrote about a lot of things, especially symbols, so this adjective, too, can be a chameleon, matching the occasion. As, "Robert Motherwell?" (You get a quick flash that he is a painter.) "I find Motherwell's later work more insistently Jungian in mood." Suppose it turns out that he was a playwright. No matter. "Work" is broad enough to cover anything.

☞ **symbolism.** Granddaddy of them all. Anything can be a symbol for something else, right? Apply to the most obvious works, imply that others are just too dense to see it. "What I admire about Wyeth is his whitewashed symbolism."

☞ **gestalt.** (geh-shtallt′). A handy little word, reeking of foreign culture, again overapplied in the forties and fifties, but still applicable to any work. It has something to do with the structure of the work. "I deplore Ionesco's despair, however much I admire the gestalt that shaped it."

☞ **kinetic** A good word for movement or motion, handy for anything you happen to like, except, say, an inert dog. Just praise the "kinetic strength" of a performance and you mean it seems to you it really grooves. Should someone suggest acidly that Beckett's plays (which must have been what they were talking about while you were dozing, daydreaming, or groping) are practically inert, you recover by pointing out that it is their very *lack* of motion that makes them so tense and therefore kinetic.

☞ **inchoate** (in-ko′ it). Equally useful for anything you happen *not* to like. "Well, I see what Durrell was driving at, but I found his *Quartet* inchoate." Which means, simply, it lacked form or coherence.

☞ **simplistic.** The same sort of word, but—simpler. To say that the artist was just not very subtle is bad-mouthing him indeed. Most effective when applied to the most abstruse of complicated works: "Empson's recent critiques are simplistic in the extreme."

☞ **plastic.** Still another put-down, much used but especially effective in referring to plastic Presidents, plastic rock music, etc. Characters in a play, novel, or libretto, or a new building, a film or book of poetry, can all be dismissed as "plastic." If you want to be clever, use the trade names of specific plastics. As, "His surfaces are pure Formica." "She moves with all the grace of polyurethane foam." Or: "I haven't seen better since Bakelite."

☞ **epiphany.** A word James Joyce picked up from his religious days and bequeathed to all literary critics. You may use more broadly: a sudden revelation or perception about the essential meaning of something. How satisfying, for example, to look at an Ellsworth Kelly diamond, spray-painted on a six-foot rectangle of canvas, and declare: "An epiphany of the struggle for balance in a world gone mad." Lay it on 'em.

Handy words, all of them, the sort that will get you through an entire weekend. If this becomes too easy you can also have fun by creating The Grand Meaningless Pronouncement. Remember the rules. First, it must be wholly irrelevant. Second, unprovable. Third, it should dazzle but at the least must puzzle. Think of the first law of higher education: You cannot intimidate if you're going to be clear or concise or understandable.

When we first saw Pinter's *The Caretaker* it seemed symbolic, God knows, but of what? At intermission the lobby was remarkably quiet; no one seemed ready to commit. When the lights flashed to return us to our seats, however, one man remarked—with no time left to dispute him—"Strangest allegory of the Crucifixion I ever saw."

Pinter, incidentally, is God's gift to flatulent phrase-droppers because he never explains the meaning of his plays—so your opinion is just as valid as Clive Barnes's or John Simon's. After seeing *The Homecoming* a lady psychologist silenced us with: "How brilliantly he exploits the ancient concept of The Mother as universal whore." Now, of course, that's part of *our* equipment.

You can make up idiot profundities of your own, such as:

• "I sense that all his disciplines are disintegrating."

• "He deals with such a restricted palette."

• "The whole lacks esprit, somehow."

• "Affecting, yes, but so *derivative*."

• "It had the delicate balance of tensions that I admire."

• "The dramatic elements are somehow lost in his overwhelming need to communicate."

• "The quality of his sensibilities was transfigured by the urgency of his vision."

At times, declarations can be accomplished by comparisons, which are particularly striking if the comparisons really make no sense:

• "The Respighi was particularly beautiful tonight, I thought. It had the light and shadow of a De Sica film."

• "Pasolini's characters all have the sweet naïveté of Prince Mishkin."

One solid device is to ignore the present performance and refer instead to another at a different time and place. You have heard someone say sniffily that he preferred the London production of a particular play. Instead of just saying "London," however, use the names

of specific theaters: "Yes, I saw it last year at the
Haymarket"—or the Royal Court or Covent Garden.
Or say you much preferred the German version at the
Stadttheater in Stuttgart. A domestic switch is to say
that you saw a much better play on the same theme in
Boston, but it closed before reaching New York. The
provincial critics didn't understand it.

Assert that the Rembrandts at the Hermitage are
the finest anywhere. Maybe they are, maybe not. Point
is that many people have been to the Louvre or to the
Rijksmuseum in Holland, but few have seen the Hermitage in Leningrad.

Particularly useful are the festivals. Everyone
comes out of the opera house raving and you simply
say, "It was nice. Although Glyndebourne did a much
better job with it two years ago." Or, "The Philhar-
monic was, as usual, adequate, but I heard that ora-
torio sung at Salzburg and it-was-the-experience-of-a-
lifetime."

Festivals to remember:

IN THIS COUNTRY

The Berkshire Festival at Tanglewood, Massa-
chusetts. Music.
Jacob's Pillow, Massachusetts. Dance.
Aspen Music Festival, Colorado.
Ojai Festival, California. Music.
Chautauqua, New York. Opera, plays, concerts.

ABROAD

Bayreuth, Germany. Wagner Festival.
Salzburg, Austria. Mozart Festival.

Edinburgh Festival, Scotland. Opera, ballet, concerts, plays.

Spoleto, Italy. Opera, ballet, concerts, plays.

Glyndebourne, England. Opera.

Dubrovnik Festival, Yugoslavia. Opera, ballet, concerts, plays.

You now have enough approaches to move easily through a cocktail party, dropping a name, muttering of a place, referring to the past. A pretentious word here, a dogmatic statement there, an enigmatic allusion in between, and you can tie up discussions in circle after circle, leaving all present awed, a little afraid, a trifle envious.

Occasionally you will get carried away and pass magisterial judgments on artists or performers that someone sophisticated will challenge, and perhaps even refute. In that case, produce this all-purpose, hit-and-run line—"You have a point. But as Aristotle said in the *Poetics,* 'El mimesis eine psysiologhikon enstikton' [Ell mee'mee-sees ay'neh phiz-ee-oh-lo-gee-kon' en'stik-ton]." This phrase translates roughly as "Imitation is an instinct of nature."

Never provide the translation until asked.

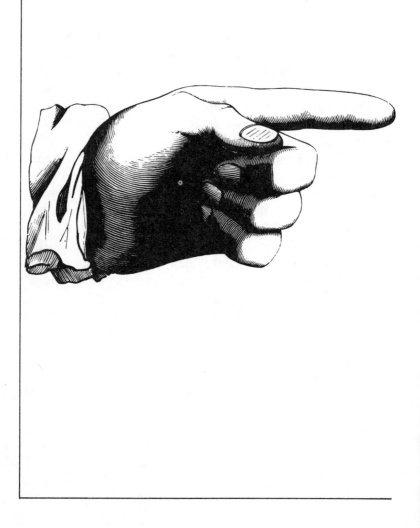

9

WHEN IT'S OPAL-NOODLING TIME IN COOBER PEDY

In several fields, even we experienced phrase-droppers find it hard to score. Sports and movies come to mind—too many people know too much. So it is with restaurants, food, and sex—everyone owns a dozen cookbooks, avidly samples the newest bistro, the latest sex manual. Travel is equally competitive.

Can you imagine anyone trying to impress his neighbors any more with slides of Piazza San Marco? Or even Machu Picchu? If Aunt Helen hasn't been to Persepolis, she's going in September and she's *been* to Katmandu. When you discover a place, the tour buses are coming around the corner.

But this system is not meant to solve only the easy ones. Though travel is an overly cultivated field, we have just the fertilizer for it.

Again, remember the basics. The rule of obscurity must prevail. You just have to go one better. Winter vacations, for instance, in the Caribbean. The Nassau, Jamaica, Virgin Islands crowd (it's hard to believe that St. John's was once an ample retort to those who had wintered in St. Thomas) hasn't a chance. They will be swamped by the Petit St. Vincent, St. Kitts, Grenada, and Cancun people. What of you, who for various uninteresting reasons never got farther than Lake Winnepesaukee (or Lake Michigan or Tahoe)?

Study a map of the Caribbean with a magnifying glass. When you find an island almost impossible to make out, you've got it made. "The hotel was primitive, but there's just nothing like snorkeling in the waters off Anguilla." Or fishing off Punta Carnero (Ecuador).

Mexico—especially Acapulco—has become routine for winter watering. Puerto Vallarta *was* less obvious, a touch more chic, but it has had too much publicity since *Night of the Iguana* and Elizabeth Taylor's choice of it for getaways. Your reply to anyone clucking about his or her two weeks at either resort is that yes, nice, although you much prefer the beaches at Playa Las Gatas. If the brash ask, "Where the hell is that?" touch the point of the épée to the middle of the breast: "Directly across from Playa La Ropa." If they haven't attacked you bodily by then, explain that both beaches are in Zihuatanejo (zee-huah-tah-nay'ho)— and *that* is halfway between the two better-known strands.

The day is not too far off when no inch of ocean-lapped sand in the Western Hemisphere will have escaped cheeky American barefoot boys, so it is well to prepare yourself. Few of your acquaintances will have seen the Seychelles, that obscure cluster of ninety-two small islands a thousand miles east of Zanzibar in the Indian Ocean. So? When the chitchat begins about the splendid beaches at Puerto Colombia or wherever, you can—with 99 per cent safety—launch into a panegyric about "the palm-fringed Beau Vallon, the utterly fantastic pleasure beach of Mahé, and"—don't even *pause* to give them a chance to interrupt—"the glories of the Vallée de Mai nature preserve, on the outer island of Praslin, so perfect that General Gordon—Gordon of Khartoum, of course—thought it might have been the original Eden."

Thus, the trick: be ready to go one better. Mrs. Bore is raving about Majorca and Ibiza; extol the beauties of Tenerife. Harry the salesman has traveled to Portugal—probably a package deal—and is likely to have seen Nazaré and the Algarve. He hasn't gone "to the untouched medieval town of Monsaraz." Neither have you—but you're on top. Someone has just returned from a camera safari to Kenya? Counter. "Of course you also went to Ruanda and Burundi."

(There's usually a newly emerging African nation that nobody's been to yet, often with good reason.)

Africa is good for points, as is, to a lesser degree, the Pacific. People have been to Japan, or swung into Hong Kong, but they do not see everything or remember enough. Not enough to prevent you from invoking the Temple of a Thousand Images or the tranquillity of the gardens of Katsura Villa. (Both are in Kyoto, Japan; the former a temple with a thousand gilded statues of Buddha, the latter the imperial summer residence used only a few times a year for moon watching while tea drinking.)

Recall how moved you were by "the somber, unchanging lives of the Floating People" (the 10,000-plus souls who live on sampans and junks outside Hong Kong). Toss into the conversation the thought that a painting or a play, even someone's dress, is as "stylized and formal as *tanka*." When they ask you what *that* means, say, "It's quite similar to *haiku*—you know, the traditional Japanese form of poetry."

In your own, genuine travels, keep your eyes and ears open, programming material for later retrieval. Though you may go to only the most traveled, trammeled places, always read the local papers, glance at a local map, pick up a detail or two for your first-aid kit.

Safer than Japan these days is Australia. Few Americans go there, and that's what makes it so valuable. Think of "I'll never forget sunset at that little sheep station in Goulburn." Or laugh with pleasure at your recollection of "the fair dinkum weekend we spent noodling at Coober Pedy" (Aussie slang for prospecting for gemstones and chips in Australia's opal mining district). *That* should knock off any snob who's been raving about the Gritti in Venice. It *is* a first-rate hotel—but who needs *him* to tell you?

When it comes to hotels and restaurants abroad, the best approach is to put down the grand establishments as too exploited. Speak out in favor of the little spot, your discovery. "Oh, I agree the Excelsior is a marvelously run hotel—though it has slipped a bit, wouldn't you agree?" (Every hotel has slipped a bit since slavery fell out of fashion.) "But last time over, we discovered a *pensione* near the Pinciana where the canopied beds are from the seventeenth century and the *donna* who owns the place makes the best *vitello tonnato* in Rome."

Or, "Yes, of course the Petite Auberge at Noves is superb, but the last time there we had trouble getting in and drove only a few kilometers to Meyrargues, where we had a meal—a meal? im*pos*sible to describe it as a mere meal—at the Château. I can't understand why Michelin gives it only two stars."

Refer not to cities but to districts. For all their Hertzing around, Americans seldom absorb the names of English counties or French provinces. Say you drove through Northumberland and let your listeners guess where you were. Rave about the cuisine of the Midi or the lesser-known wines of Gascony. Praise the inns of the Brabant and leave the listener wondering. . . . ("Is that France . . . Holland, or Belgium?")

Obscure locale is one approach. Obscurity *within* a place is another. If everyone is chattering about Italy, how they adore the Giotto frescoes at Padua or the *gelati* of Amalfi or the tailors of Milan, move quietly but boldly back to Rome itself and rave about (1) the fountains at Piazza Braschi (which few guidebooks bother to mention), (2) the Caravaggio Madonna at the Agostino Church (where few tourists stop), or (3) the divine *saltimbocca* at La Carbonara, a restaurant no American ever entered before. (If someone says he has, chuckle at your slip and say you meant the Carabinieri, naturally—a restaurant that even fewer have gone to, since it doesn't exist.) The same game can be played in any city, obviously, and though it is a nuisance to ferret out such places, you only need one or two and it is no more troublesome and much more useful than taking roll upon roll of film.

Handy and quick—drop not the name of the city; drop its airport. One does it automatically when talking of travels in this country—"I came into Kennedy," "We landed at Dulles," etc. Such easy familiarity with the world's airports makes for easy, worldly, airborne conversation. You didn't stop over in Paris for the weekend, you "came into Orly Friday night and left from De Gaulle Monday morning." (Orly handles international flights and De Gaulle continental flights.) The same sort of switch holds for London. Heathrow is the airport most people see, but Gatwick is like London's La Guardia, serving local flights, and it's worth a half point to drop it into conversation. Keep in mind the following:

Copenhagen	Kastrup
Vienna	Schwechat
Amsterdam	Schiphol
Madrid	Barajas
Athens	Ellinikon
Stockholm	Arlanda
Berlin	Tempelhof
Bangkok	Don Muang
Hong Kong	Kai Tak

Talking about airlines and even airplanes can be a splendid way of showing your familiarity with the routine of world travel. "I prefer Aer Lingus' service to London just because their terminals are less crowded, you know." Or, "I fly Viscounts whenever I can. So much quieter." Or, as one man I know is fond of repeating, "The Caravelle is a fantastic plane. It's like a Frenchwoman—all the power is in the tail."

If all else fails, reverse snobbery is probably the only answer. I recall a neighbor of mine who listened quietly at the first cocktail party of the fall as couple after couple recounted their wanderings abroad, their hotel and restaurant discoveries, their brilliant purchases in the flea markets of the world. At the least, they boasted about the vast decks of the beach houses they had occupied. Finally it occurred to someone present that my neighbor Jim had been silent. "Jim," he was approached, "what did you and Harriet do this summer?"

Jim handled it beautifully. "We stayed home and screwed a lot." Or, if bluntness is not your bag, just smile and say that you and Jo decided to explore each other, and really use the house, stayed off the beach and off the planes and off the sauce and pressures.

As the conversation and faces turn to you, feed it a little. "We took time off as we felt like it, slept late, read, relaxed, puttered around in the garden, puttered around in the city. Saw some theater—no trouble getting tickets—had several good meals—the restaurants were empty—and it was great."

And now, as the world travelers sink slowly into the west, let us turn to the foreigners themselves. . . .

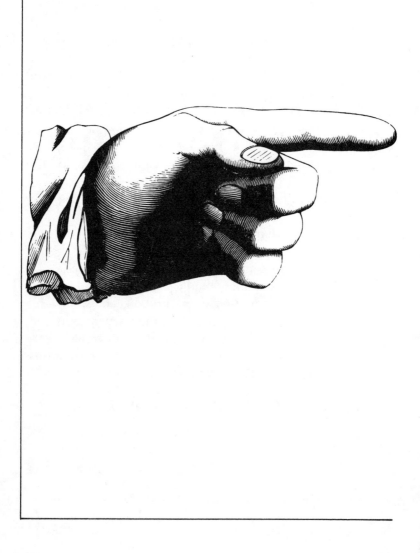

10
DEALING WITH FOREIGNERS— LIKE YOURSELF:
A Footnote on Travel

One's fellow Americans may be difficult, but confronting Europeans can be nothing short of humiliating. We are still callow, naïve, and frontier-raw in their eyes. Bellboys at the better hotels look us over with hauteur. The concierge is condescending, the maître d' the master of our fate. Enough!

A friend has come up with a simple ploy. It rests on the fact that educated people abroad usually converse in English when Americans are present. They assume—often correctly—that your command of their tongue is feeble or non-existent, and they pride themselves on their command of yours. So if you talk English and then, in mid-sentence, deliver the precisely appropriate *mot*, you will have gained, if not the upper hand, at least one upper cut.

Our friend George browses through a French-English (or German-English, Italian-English, or Spanish-English) dictionary until he comes to one or two words he has never seen but which look esoteric and exotic and which he is reasonably certain he can, with practice, pronounce properly. Then he is ready.

George, who is a prominent editor, once dined at the home of Raoul, a French publisher. Raoul disguised —thinly—his patronizing attitude toward all things American. He could not quite conceal his contempt, though he tried. George might, after all, be a conduit of cash to the Parisian's own bank account—and, to a Frenchman, money is above contempt.

When he casually asked George's view of the most important book on his fall list, *Rasputin the Divine*, George was prepared with a *fait de faire tourner les tables*. He stared thoughtfully at the ceiling for a moment, then said, "Beyond doubt, Raoul, it is a good book, a fine book. Perhaps a brilliantly innovative work. Yet I must tell you that certain portions—

Chapter 22, for example, and the last four paragraphs of Chapter 48—are for me [pause] *indéchiffrable* [aan-day-she-frah-bl]."*

Raoul was visibly shaken. Putting down his wine-glass, he murmured, "I beg your pardon?"

"*Indéchiffrable*—or should I say . . . *indébrouillable* [aan-day-broo-yabl]?"†

This time George saw the Frenchman blanch. The double-barreled barrage had worked beautifully: George had him in his own precious tongue. A splendid moment for ego and America.

On another occasion in Paris, George scored big off the well-known French *snobbisme* about wine. His French host had ordered, with lots of fuss and frowning deliberation, a vintage Margaux. He was clearly out to show this Pepsi-guzzling colonial. George sipped, swallowed, smiled a beatific smile. "Aaah," he murmured, "*comme le petit Jésus en culottes de velours* [like the Christ child in velvet pants]!" He had used a phrase not one American in ten million is expected to know.

The Frenchman almost gagged with astonishment. "But, monsieur, you speak *excellent* French!"

George made a slight gesture of deprecation and delivered a French idiom which was the knockout blow: "*Je parle français comme une vache espagnole* [I speak French like a Spanish cow]. In fact," he murmured, "I know only a few phrases."

Which is God's honest truth, but he will never be believed. Nor will you.

But what, you say, if you are going not to France or Spain or Yugoslavia but to England? The English

* *Undecipherable, incomprehensible.*
† Inexplicable, cannot be unraveled.

have their own well-bred contempt for "foreigners," which includes several of their queens, most continentals, all colonials, and their own King George I, the Hanoverian.

Language can work here, too, but it requires colloquialisms. Many of them you know.

"Lay on" means to arrange for.

"Knock up" means to awaken someone.

"Saloon" is a sedan model car, and the "boot," of course, is the trunk of a car.

"Post" is what we call "mail."

Put them all together and your conversation could lull a Limey into dropping his guard. Or chin.

"Simpson's made all the room arrangements by post and I've laid on the transport. I've booked a Humber saloon; despite all we're taking, there'll be plenty of room for the parcels in the boot. But we'd best get an early start. I've asked the hall porter to knock us up at seven."

A bit much, perhaps, but you get the idea.

It is also beneficial to bone up on English history —for a paragraph or two. The British cherish their glorious past above all else, though many may be fuzzy on details; too much precision they consider Germanic pedantry. So a *little* historical precision—with finesse—can accomplish much, especially when it comes from so unexpected a source as an American.

When his British hosts took our friend George to Glastonbury Abbey, for example, they expected the usual trite expressions of awe or mumbling about King Arthur. Instead, George said, "Ah *yes*, this is as far as Monmouth got, as I remember, before they nabbed him in Hampshire." His friends knew the Duke of Monmouth figured somewhere but weren't quite sure if he was a Lancastrian or a Yorkist or neither. Somehow the conversation shifted quickly to the lush countryside around the abbey. One fact had won the day.

A smattering of history is helpful; combined with Shakespeare, it is wicked. Before a visit to the Tower of London with some distant English cousins, George spent a few minutes with his Penguin edition of Shakespeare's plays. Once inside the Tower dungeons, he paused, folded his hands, and looked down silently for a second. The cousins were pleased; silence denoted to them a proper American humility. Then George intoned: "Their lips were four red roses on a stalk/Which in their summer beauty kiss'd each other."

"Eh? What's that?" said one cousin.

"Oh," said George, "just the Bard on the two little princes, of course. Act IV of *Richard III*—Scene 3, wasn't it?"

The perfect way to subdue the sceptred isle.

11
WHY JOHNNY GETS D's— FOR DYSLEXIA

Only at dinner parties of swinging singles or ailing ancients does the subject of children and their progress in school fail to arise. Not that education in itself is so fascinating. Except possibly for an Adult Education class in crewel work, tennis, or Commodity Futures for the Beginner (or the Wiped-Out), most of us could not be dragged back into a classroom. And we don't want to talk about it.

But many children from five to twenty-five are in school, and in a day of advanced degrees, kindergarten graduations, and towering tuitions, one must expect the talk, like the tab, to go on forever. The problem gets worse. Everything has been said. It becomes aggravated if the guests are old friends. "How is Howard getting along with Miss Murtagh this year?" Then a pause, and the effort not to sound too snide: "Is there still . . . uh . . . a discipline problem?"

At another level: "Did Sandy graduate from Smith in June? Or was she joining that ashram in India? I've forgotten."

Mothers are at it all day long, talking to other mothers. At least the young matron, restless in domesticity, can feel she is involved in the destiny of her brood and, thereby, of the nation. But fathers too get involved, falling into the subject at business lunches: "That goddam school . . . Patricia is nine now and she can't multiply 7 times 8 without gazing at the ceiling for five minutes."

It's enough to drive a man to drink—the *other* man, across the table.

Discussions about education become heated because most parents are compensating for the vacillation of their own views. We no sooner see the wisdom of "training the young for real life" than we become panicked because the three R's are being neglected. Should education be vocational—or a "rounded" preparation? Forget it. Take an Olympian view and interject into these grand debates a few universal observations spoken with the tone of great authority. Say it the way professionals say it and your fellow laymen will listen —or, better still, shut up.

If the group is arguing about how math is taught these days, you could say, "Say what you like, I'm still a firm believer in the *core curriculum*." Eh? What's that? Patiently explain. This approach combines different subjects in the same class time—math, therefore, could be taught with science, English with social studies. "Train the youngsters to cross-fertilize knowledge. Why shouldn't *A Tale of Two Cities* be read in history class?"

Mrs. Botts is concerned that little Lance is the youngest in his class? "It's one of the reasons," say you, "that I favor the *alternative classroom*." Again, if necessary, elucidate. The phrase means what it says, more or less—some alternative to the standard classroom setup: multi-age groupings in the same classroom, for example, which might settle Lance's problem, or the melding of two third grades, retaining two teachers in the same room, which might settle his hash. *Alternative teaching* is an alternative buzz word.

Should the discussion swing over to the difficulties modern-day schools face—students under greater stress to perform, growing numbers of students troubled by broken homes, drugs, schools struggling to cope with the demands of minority groups, budgets, move in with: "What's needed today to meet such strains is more *individualization*, a *multidisciplinary approach* to problems of *behavior modification*."

If you must translate: "Individualization" is a Germanic way of saying teachers should try to make instruction personal, individual, relate it to the capacity of each child. A most up-to-date approach. Also, the same one practiced in the one-room schoolhouse. A "multidisciplinary approach" to problem solving means simply that school administrators, teachers, and the school psychologist work together when faced with a difficult student, rather than leaving it to one teacher alone. "Behavior modification" almost explains itself: changing the way Dick and Jane act (especially if they keep disappearing into the closet).

Now for several simple phrases to pull you through the rough spots:

Remember *affective domain*. Impressive, yes? "However education is approached, it must strive to create an affective domain." That's educator talk for an environment conducive to learning.

More personally, when they begin talking about their own offspring, remember that one-upmanship usually rests on simple competition. Whose kid is getting the best grades? If your baby Barbra (age seventeen) is still bringing home A's, you just brag away, softly, with the others. But if young Dustin is *not* at the top of the class—is, in fact, struggling for survival near the bottom—you have a choice. (A) Retreat into shameful silence or (B) put a bold face on it. How? The right words, once again. In addition: remember that no child is dumb any more. Kids have *learning problems*.

A child is slow in learning to read? Never fear. "Karen seems to be afflicted with a certain degree of *dyslexia*." (It means, loosely, a reading problem.)

Similarly, if the kid's flunking math, attribute it to "a mild case of *dyscalculia*." Or if the kid can't write legibly, put it down to *dysgraphia*.

Some children, sadly, suffer from very real medical, muscular, mental, generic, or cultural shortcomings. They and their parents deserve sympathy. But, in other cases, how easy to soften unpleasant reality with a medical-sounding diagnosis, as though the child had measles. If the kid has a *learning disability*, he's not stupid; it becomes like any other disability—something God willed. Using the jargon establishes that the parent, at least, is a brain.

Now if the child is doing badly in *every* subject, and you even suspect he or she may be just plain out of it, don't give up, at least in public. Four possible approaches:

• "We feel he is basically a bright child, but at the moment he is suffering a *developmental lag.*"

• "The brains are there, all right, but Trish has problems in the *cognitive* area." (Which means Trish knows 2 plus 2 equals 4 but can't figure out that 4 *minus* 2 comes out to 2.)

• "Sarah would be getting top grades, really, if she weren't having a bit of trouble with *conceptualization.*" (Sarah can learn by rote but can't grasp underlying principles and apply them to other situations. She knows that 2 *apples* and 2 *apples* are 4—but tangerines drive her bananas.)

• "Howard's as smart as any kid in the class, but he's *hypoactive.*" That's a word for sluggish and unresponsive. More crudely, it can mean lazy. Hypoactive is double strength because most people will think you've said hyperactive.

Hyperactive or *hyperkinetic* is the opposite, a hopped-up kid who can't concentrate, who when asked to recite does forty laps around the classroom.

If the kid is kicked out, apply a verbal palliative. "Yes, we thought it best if Harvey left the school for now. He really is an *exceptional child.*" (You bet!) "But the school and I just couldn't come to an agreement about *behavioral objectives.*"

You will not always be totally successful. Others may snicker a bit, and meanwhile the kid is still at home, scrawling blueprints to blow up the school. But at least when there is no perfect word for him, you can enjoy the solace of having the last one.

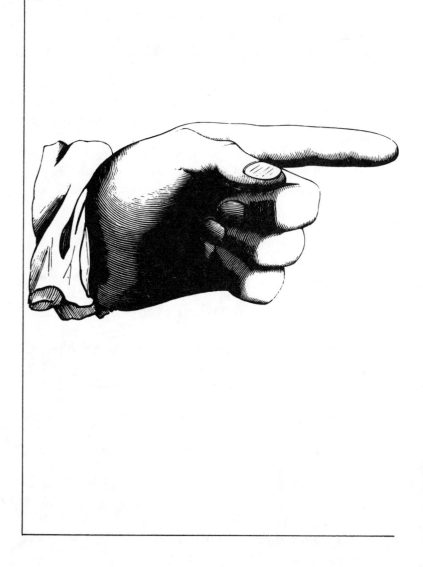

12
WORDS
MOTHER
NEVER
TAUGHT
YOU:
A Gallimaufry
of Goodies

Even if we forget the idiot buzz words, the latest insider language in the fields of finance or falconry, pure vocabulary, as Miss Curtis in sixth grade always taught us, can be a powerful ally. Just plain words—or not so plain words—can stun. An impressive vocabulary is . . . well, impressive, especially if nicely underplayed.

That does not mean you should memorize arcane words or try to overwhelm with "ten-dollar words." The ten-cent variety will serve. The person who puffs up to utter, "The differential is not substantive," instead of saying, "There isn't much difference," will be put down as a pompous pain.

And devilishly obscure words winnowed from dictionaries or overwriters are of little use either. We know one young woman who puts a check mark in the margin of a book whenever she comes across an unfamiliar word, then looks it up and tries to "put it into practice in everyday life."

After reading Nabokov's *Ada*, for example, she asked her date at the movies if they could sit in the entresol (mezzanine), complained that the film was acarpous (sterile), then apologized for her post-movie borborygmus (rumbling stomach). When her date offered to assuage it with a snack and subsequently complimented her on the pin she was wearing, she said it was a mere eburnean breloque (ivory trinket) and that he had very nice prasine eyes. Old Green Eyes went away and never called again.

This kind of self-improvement stuff is really only effective to nick someone who is showing off a presumably dazzling vocabulary. Suppose she stops you in midsentence to say, "Excuse me, but you said 'mental telepathy.' 'Mental telephathy' is a redundancy." It is of some small satisfaction to say, "Of course—patently a pleonasm" (a synonym for redundancy).

Or if someone smirks, "She's a daughter of Lesbos, you know," it makes the moment to shake your head and demur: "Not so much tribadic [Lesbian] as epicene [having the characteristics of both sexes], I think."

Or if a mutual friend is described, since her divorce, as "having turned into a veritable anchorite," a useful Buckleyesque rejoinder is, "Yes, as eremitic [hermit-like] as a stylite [a solitary ascetic]." Which is a trifle pleonastic, though no one will notice.

But these are special cases, buckshot to send a small bore on his way. A more functional everyday tactic is to use naggingly familiar words, ones first heard defined in school, the kind that crop up in multiple-choice exams. We come across them in our reading and guess their meaning from the context, but we haven't really looked them up since tenth grade. There's the point: anyone who uses them with self-assurance is a bit impressive, rather than trying to impress. Others will realize that such words should be in the ordinary intellectual baggage of those with even a commonplace education. *They know they should know.*

Let us construct our own little lexicon, all carefully chosen on the basis of familiarity and adaptability. Remember—they are scored as throwaways, underdone, glancing blows, not as direct hits.

solipsism (the theory that the self is the only thing we truly know exists). Not to be confused with solecism, a gaffe in speech—"They was going"—or other breach of form. "Solipsism" is handy for putting down the egotist: "Sure, Al, and that opinion, my man, is just a reflection of your solipsistic view of the world."

☞ **meretricious** (artificially and vulgarly attractive). "Of course the show is crowd-pleasing, but it's really meretricious crap." "Specious" used to be effective, but too many people know it.

☞ **sententious** (an affected use of maxims and dogmatic statements). Don't mix it up with another fine word, "tendentious," having a tendency or bias. If you have just listened to a heavily stated opinion which you are unwilling to accept but unable to combat, just smile and say, "Murray is so sententious, when at heart he's really sentimental." This is the slap-and-pat style, suggesting that Murray has a heart, but also a problem.

☞ **jejune** (dull, insipid, unsatisfying to the mind). A beautiful put-down because it covers so many weaknesses. "You really liked *Fear of Flying*? I thought it a jejune libel on feminism."

☞ **dichotomy** (dividing into parts or branches). Once was overworked, especially among academics and those who wished they were. But less familiar, and therefore more effective, is the adjective form: "She's the victim of her own dichotomous character, *constantly* at war with itself, and no truce in sight."

☞ **paradigm** (pattern or example). "No, Mr. Bryson, the memos aren't ready yet. On Mondays I seem to be a paradigm of lethargy." This flat but classy statement of a common human condition will leave the boss with little rejoinder. Who could fire a secretary or aide who fires off such a line?

☞ **entropy** (sameness or uniformity). Okay, so your boss *does* have a rejoinder: "You're fired." Tell friends later that you're "merely resisting the entropy of corporate life."

☞ **ataxia** (inability to coordinate; lack of orderly arrangement). A medical term, now used also in talk of educational problems, it translates nicely into other spheres. As, "I'm afraid Genevieve suffers from moral ataxia."

☞ **putative** (commonly thought or supposed). "Jennifer is six months along, and guess who's the putative papa? Her ex-husband!"

☞ **portentous** (of the nature of a portent; thus, significant of the future, but also marvelous and amazing). When asked to comment on a pundit, President, or prophet's latest economic message—which you haven't read and won't understand—look wise and weary and declare, "Portentous—really portentous—but delivered in the same old all-purpose prose. He never risks being purple."

☞ **lagniappe** (a gratuity or free extra). A delicious word, exotic, like tropical fruit, but with a simple meaning. "We paid handsomely for the house and the tennis court, so he threw in the Gravely mower—pure lagniappe."

☞ **symbiotic** (a biological term that describes two dissimilar organisms living together, usually for mutual benefit). This has had a huge vogue in conglomerating business and is now gone. Use it in other connections. Obviously the perfect word to describe the marriages of most of our friends. "Richard and Celia were made for each other—they're *completely* symbiotic, like the Marquis de Sade and O."

☞ **gallimaufry** (a hodgepodge, jumble, hash). "Her life is a gallimaufry of Vuitton, Gucci, Pucci, and Sears."

☞ **bathetic** (mawkishly sentimental, trite, trivial). A pointed pejorative, perfect for piercing any novel, play, film, or person—writers, say, who overdo alliteratives, as in this sentence.

☞ **Pharisee** (a sanctimonious hypocrite). This is one of those words—like *sybarite* (a lover of luxury),

Jacobin (a political radical), *Philistine* (a crass person motivated by material values), and *Epicurean* (one who believes the highest good in life is pleasure)—that are rich in overtones of erudition. One could wish for a dozen, but it is easy to confuse them. So stick with one, like Pharisee, which covers a multitude of sinners. Pharisaic, the adjective form, is good, too, and sounds vaguely Hebraic, which adds points.

☞ **numinous** (spiritual, wondrous, arousing elevated feelings). Lovely for your occasional word of praise. To your hostess: "Lucy, you look positively numinous." She may not know the word—or may think you mean luminous—but your evening or weekend—and hers—has been improved.

Enough. The list is long, in fact limitless. Memorize three or four.

Occasionally a person sensitive to the nuances will realize that a reversal is called for. At a recent dinner party in Shaker Heights, one man was going on about liberals who seek an accommodation with the Communist world, "when we all know that these genuflections can only result in masochistic immolation." One woman's response was eloquent: "My dear Brock, that is blatant bullshit." She was admired by all.

13
MINTING WORDS:
Pretentious Prefix and Stylish Suffix

Words come into vogue, have a certain cachet for a time (like "certain" and "cachet"), and then drop into obscurity. Timing is needed here. It's all Wall Street. Catch them on the way up, drop them before they become common parlance and unfashionably stale. It's like the Italian loafers with the horsy hardware. If you were one of the first to wear them, great. Once Thom McAn had them at $14.95, their status rating was lower than feet.

A few years ago, for instance, it was smart to echo hippie talk. You could use "dig," "bag," "rap," "out of sight," "psych out," or "rip off," and sound really "with it." (Half of it was, in fact, left over from the late jazz, especially bop, era of the forties and fifties.) Then the week came when three advertisers proclaimed a deodorant pad, a sink cleaner, and a hemorrhoid cure that "get it all together," and you knew such talk was over. If ad men are saying it, if everyone is saying it, what leverage is there in *your* saying it?

Another example is "charisma." In 1960, if someone said, "The Kennedys' esprit is amazing; they are the embodiment of what Max Weber called charisma," he would have been an impressive adversary over the brandy glasses. Now the word is as useful as a corset stay.

At times you can prolong the life of a current favorite by—remember the basics—changing context. Politicians, for example, love to go on about our present political or economic "posture"; thus, you could refer to the "cultural posture" of your local school board, or the "compensation posture" of the company's personnel department.

If others discuss the "thrust" of American policy in the Mideast, why don't you talk about the "thrust of the Washington Redskins' new backfield strategy" or "the thrust of Sylvia Porter's book on economics"?

The "parameters" of world trade are being defined in congressional addresses? Well, if you must appropriate it—deadly word—speak of the "parameters" of Marlon Brando's recent performances. A commission studying urban behavior patterns says it is looking for a "purchase" on the problem of drugs; say you are looking for a "purchase" on the problem of your backhand.

Even so, adapted words will have had their day. You need to develop your own ear for the nuances of change. For six months after Tom Wolfe coined the phrase "radical chic" it had value over the luncheon table; then it lost its potency. One smiled a bit condescendingly at the slow learner who finally tried the phrase out in public. Radical C. had become ridiculed, had turned the other chic.

A much safer method is to mint your own. Get yourself a fix—a *pre*fix. You are attending the opening of a new show at the museum. Everyone is swarming around trying to make the definitive statement about unintelligible daubs. Pick a well-known artist— Matisse, say. Ring the changes: instead of, "The composition is a lot like Matisse," try, "I'd say the composition is neo-Matisse."

Rather than, "That reminds me of Matisse," say, "The work is derivative—quasi-Matisse."

If you want to say the painter has imitated Matisse, but unsuccessfully, "pseudo Matisse," obviously. If you aren't sure of what you think, label the work "crypto-Matisse." (The Matisse element is hidden, but it's there.)

By referring everything new back to the masters (and Pissarro is better than Picasso), you will be able to say something about almost every painting. A few find it effective to murmur evaluations of the *chiaroscuro*—the use of light and shade in a picture—which impresses others who vaguely thought it was a Spanish dance. But you needn't restrict prefixes to art: they will fix things nicely for music, buildings, philosophy—anything you like. They have a dogmatic quality about them and in dogma there is strength.

Other prefixes to call upon handily include "demi," meaning "half" or "lesser" (the demigods, you recall, are the lesser deities), which works if you refer to the "demirich," the "demiliterate," or the "demisophisticated."

"Micro" and "macro" are more difficult to use fluently. "Micro," roughly, small or miniature, has been a popular high—or upper middle—brow word for a long time. Microcosm, "the world in miniature." "Micro" doesn't quite equate with "mini" but it sounds more learned. You can get away with using it loosely. As, "James is micro-educated," or "When it comes to bridge, Ginny is spontaneous but micro-skilled." "Microcephalic" might do for small-brained. "Macro," meaning, approximately, large or great, has become best known in "macrobiotics," referring to foods and diets that prolong life, or macroeconomics. But to type a current X-rated movie "macroporn" is a score.

• "Hyper" is overused; it suffers from hyperexposure. But "hypo," meaning the opposite—a hypothyroid person, you remember, needs some pepping up—has good life left in it. As:

• "Tennis? I've always been hypoathletic."

• "Frank does like his tipple, all right. You wouldn't characterize the old boy as hypoabstemious."

Another prefix, "dis," proves most helpful when used unexpectedly. You can say "diseconomy" instead of "waste," for example, or, if your diet is going well, speak of your "acquired disincentive to eat."

Using the reverse ploy, there's good fun in words

with the expected prefix left off—and all of these are
real words, honest-to-Webster's.

• "I think the Mets are vincible this year."

• "The outcome of that election is entirely evita-
ble."

• "Well, Harriet keeps what you'd call a maculate
apartment."

• "Now that the doors are open a crack, we'll see
how scrutable the Chinese really are."

• "Hank puts up a tough front, but he is eminently
domitable."

Become adept at using two simple suffixes. At-
taching "ian" or "esque" is an easy way to get much
mileage out of little knowledge. "Orwellian" everyone
knows—the kind of state-controlled world pictured in
1984. "Brechtian" is better, "Pinteresque," "Barthian,"
"Skinnerian," or "Laingian" okay if theater, literature,
or psychology is the subject. Instead of harking back to
Future Shock, a book title which long ago had its day,
call the World Trade Center, for example, "Tofflerian,"
a reference to the author.

For any subject you can't understand—or if you
haven't been listening—label the problem or situation
"Borgesian" (Bore-hay'see-an), a reference to the Ar-
gentine writer, Jorge Luis Borges, whose stories are ab-
stract, puzzling, difficult to describe or explain, sur-
realistic and, sometimes, fun.

If you want to bang off a passing reference to the
three leading exponents of brilliant befuddling, call
them the three B's. If you can draw somebody into
thinking you mean Bach, Beethoven, and Brahms, level
the landscape with "No, sorry, I meant Barth,
Barthelme, and Borges." (The first is John—called
Jack, if you want to get cute—and the second is
Donald, although he has a writing brother, Frederick, if
you want to get impossible.)

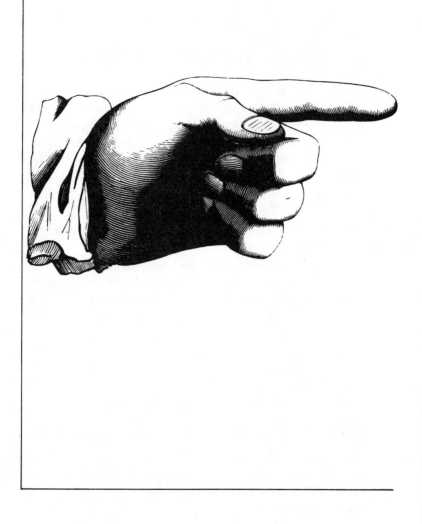

14
KEEPING UP WITH THE (DOW)JONESES

Maybe the parties you go to end up as in X-rated novels, with group orgies after dessert, but the urban or suburban gatherings most people attend follow a different pattern. The women cluster, even as their mothers did, to swap evaluations of the latest in schools, fashions, and diets, and the men huddle in another corner to discuss—what?

Well, often it's sports, and sometimes sex, and sooner or later politics, and we'll go into the Washington tribal idiom elsewhere. The other masculine area of conversation is business and the economy, which is related to Washington because money talk is frequently prefaced by much headshaking over the stupidity of "those bureaucrats."

When men talk about their own businesses the conversation becomes short bursts of monologue, for a man in frozen smorgasbits seems to have little to exchange with someone in drop forgings. So a more common ground is sought. The morning paper's figures on car sales or inventory levels or the predictions of a Yale economist are reiterated. If you find yourself lost in such dreary stuff, interrupt when you want to get in, get out, or take over by saying, "All that may be true enough, but it really depends on what the Fed does about M_1."

Only a rare bird can reply to that. Whether or not it is true is beside the point. First, anyone who refers to the Federal Reserve Board by its nickname is obviously at home in the world of economics. Second, M_1? What in blazes is M_1? Well, you explain if you must that "M_1 is the money supply measured by cash in circulation and in checking accounts, while M_2 includes money in time deposits."

The conversation will surely shift. Who would want to go further into the subject with you around?

The topic that usually follows is the stock market. This subject too may be rapidly shut off or turned. For when the market is going up, most men are too superstitious to brag that United Potato has tripled in six months for fear that United will plunge ten points in the next ten hours. And if the market is going down, they are loath to admit what fools they have made of themselves, to own up to the sinking fear they experience reading the fine print over breakfast, the orange juice churning in their gullets. So they mumble, yes, the market's been crummy, hasn't it?

Only one type will talk freely. These are the geniuses who always buy at the bottom and sell at the top and who pick nothing but winners. Don't be intimidated for a minute. They are lying. They deserve a proper put-down. Prepare a few in advance.

☞ **Prevaricator:** "I know the market's been lousy, but I've been lucky. Friend at the club touted me on International Aggregates, and I've picked up twenty points in a couple of months. Only wish I had bought more than 5,000 shares."

☞ **You:** "Oh, you latched onto IAG too. I liked the stock early on—my charts led me to it—and I really plunged. Didn't want to tie up too much cash, so I bought options. A bundle of them. Tremendous leverage."

Now this short rejoinder employs three effective elements. First, call a stock by its symbol rather than by its real name. If you want to play dirty keep a *Standard & Poor's Stock Guide* at home, and before any party check the newspaper for the names of three big winners of the day before, then look up their ticker-tape symbols in the *S & P Guide*. (See how, even here, initials suggest long familiarity with the subject?) Drop these symbols casually into the conversation. Instead of Westinghouse, say WX, or EK instead of Eastman Kodak—and it is obvious that you are on intimate terms with the market.

Another gambit: use the nicknames of stocks instead of their symbols, where possible—"Ma Bell" for A T & T, "Pennsy" for Penn Central, "Big Steel" for U. S. Steel, "Becky" for Beckman Instruments, and our favorite, "Mickey Mouse" for Disney Productions. It sounds very inside to say, "I've always believed in special situations. I wouldn't touch a number like Bessie [Bethlehem Steel]."

Second, note the reference to charting. Few people know what chartists do, and even when their work is explained it retains a mysterious quality, like alchemy. "My point and figure work told me to dump Specious Commodities in the high 80s," and your reputation for Street savviness is made.

A variation is a reference to the "odd-lot index," the indicator that charts the investment sentiment of those without sufficient capital to buy a "round lot," or 100 shares—that is, the public at large. If you say, "The odd-lot index convinced me the market had peaked and I moved into cash and commercial paper"—jab, feint, and uppercut. "Commercial paper," "Treasury bills," and "CDs" (certificates of deposit), all ways to invest cash for the short term, will intimidate or wipe out all of your listeners who make less than a hundred big ones a year.

Third, of course, is your reference to options. No need to explain them here, or indeed to understand what they are in any case. You could say you bought "puts" or "calls" but that is dangerous, because you are too likely to get confused and say "puts" when you should say "calls" and "calls" when you should say "puts." Just use "options," which covers both. Then throw in "leverage," and you imply that you know how to make a fortune on a shoestring by clever borrowing.

If the group concludes the market is hard to figure right now (which is almost all the time), say, "That's why I've been buying straddles." A straddle is a put *and* a call, apparently a brilliant response to indecision.

There are a couple of other flag words that can be substituted. But always use "leverage": "Oh yes, I had some Rorschach Unlimited, I'm happy to say. Bought the warrants. More leverage."

Never mind whether or not Rorschach ever *issued* warrants. He won't know either.

Another possibility: "PSO? Yes, indeed, that one has been very good to me, ver-r-ry good. I took a big position in the converts. Better leverage. Worked out beautifully."

Again, it doesn't matter whether or not the company put out convertible bonds once or in 1923, or never. The point is that steady tapping with the words "options," "warrants," and "convertibles" will dent ninety-nine out of a hundred people. They have heard of them, but they don't *quite* know what they are, and they have almost certainly never traded them. (You must always be sure, of course, that there are no brokers or real money managers present. This guide is for middle-level chatter.)

The jargon of the trade not only marks you as superior to other men but it can be helpful in camouflaging your precarious personal financial state. Isn't it better to claim you are "employing leverage" than to admit you have borrowed to the hilt? In the first instance men will respect your business sense, but if you say you owe everyone in town you're a bum.

Avoid the word "money." Too common. Instead, substitute "assets" or "capital." Again, how much more dignified, if you are broke, to say, "I am temporarily short of working capital." This is poverty at a higher level.

Referring to your debts as "liabilities" helps too. If the bank won't grant you a loan you can always blame "tight money" for shutting down your "line of credit." If in desperation you take your Christmas Club money out in July, tell yourself that you are merely "tapping contingent reserves." One man we know is *always* borrowing from his family, but he puts a bold face on insolvency by declaring, "I have taken the option of refunding my obligations with a fresh instrument of debt."

Eschew the plebeian. Refer to stocks as "common stocks," as though you are just as likely to own uncommon ones (that is, preferreds). Better yet, say "equities." A highly versatile word, "equity" can be substituted for "ownership" whenever business is under discussion. Rather than concede, "Yes, I own about half my house now, and the bank, bless it, is sitting on the other half," declare, "Yes, my equity in the place is now around the 50 per cent level." A bit pompous perhaps, but you are evidently a man of affairs, one given to lunching in fortieth-floor private dining rooms, and therefore such formalisms are inevitable.

If you own more than one stock, talk about your "portfolio." If there are any bonds in that portfolio, call them "debentures" instead. Sure, there's a difference, but not one person in a million really knows what it is, and "debenture" sounds so much more impressive. Instead of saying you have been buying or selling stocks or bonds, say, "I've taken a position" or "I've been fine-tuning my portfolio."

The New York Stock Exchange is always the "Big Board," and the American Stock Exchange the "Amex." And forever cite as your authority either "the pros" or "the institutions." Whoever they may be—and they are just as wrong as the rest of us—a reference to what the pros or the big institutions think will sway multitudes.

"Liquidity" is handy. Instead of: "I've been selling lately," say, "I've been moving to a more liquid position." If you are heading for the bankruptcy courts, preserve your stature by proclaiming, "I am currently undergoing a liquidity crisis." You are now on a par with Penn Central, W. T. Grant, and other corporations once worth billions.

Other stock market words much bandied about are "price-earnings ratio," which you can just call a p/e, and "beta." The p/e, also called the "multiple," is the number you get when you divide the current price of the stock by what each share earned last year. "Beta" is a new computer measurement; it rates the riskiness of a stock by its volatility in recent trading. Stocks with high p/e's also tend to have high betas, so it's easy to say, "When the discount rate started to go up, I got concerned and lightened up on some of my high p/e stocks. You know, lessens the beta factor."

One final hint about the market. This one never fails when the boys are either chortling over the market's recent rise—oops, bullishness—or groaning over fresh losses. You say, in the first instance, "I'm locking in my gains," and, in the second, "I had already hedged myself before the drop." If they're still conscious, pause and add: "I've been selling against the box."

Don't ask. The explanation has something to do with being both long and short in the same stock at the same time, but now you'll be wanting a definition of "long" and "short." It really doesn't matter. Even if they've heard of it—even if they understand it—the chances are very slim that they have *done* it. As far as they are concerned, solvent, insolvent, liquid, solid, faker or fakir, you too are a "pro."

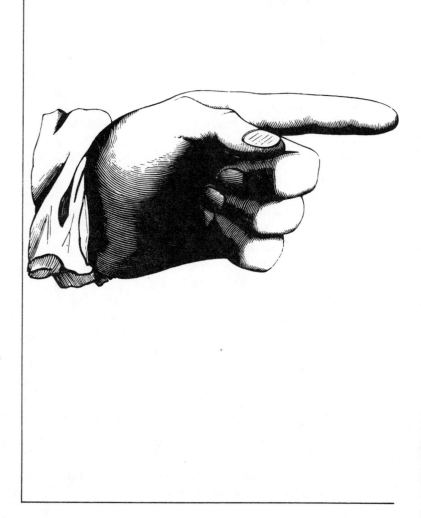

15
WE'RE OFF
ON THE
ROAD TO
CANOSSA

The venerable is venerated. All of us can talk about what's in the papers this week. Some of us can remember details about what was in the papers ten years ago, and such people command respect. But if you can go further back in history you have it made. The further the better. And somehow—as we said about Latin—knowledge of the classical period still impresses most of us. That's *real* education, the kind they dispensed at Groton and St. Mark's while the rest of us were studying Spanish at P.S. 84. The Past has Class.

Of course, you don't want to go back and actually read Plutarch, Thucydides, Bulfinch, Gibbon, and *The Golden Bough.* Heavens, no! There's a much easier way to make it appear that these rarefied regions are your natural habitat: just familiarize yourself with some of the following classical and historical allusions and cast them into the conversation like pearls before kine.*

☞ **Augean, or Augean stables.** Greek legend has it that King Augeas kept three thousand oxen for thirty years without cleaning the stables, so you can see why a reference to Augean suggests a fantastic mess. Hercules, using brain as well as brawn, cleaned them up by diverting a river through them, thus creating one of the earliest examples of water pollution. Ergo: "The job I'm facing with that Swinnerton deal is positively Augean—and I don't feel much like Hercules on Mondays." Any backbreaking task will sound more so if dubbed *Herculean.*

☞ **King Charles's head.** The English can't get over the fact that one of their kings was decapitated. It's such an un-English thing to have happened, something

---

* You thought it was swine, right? Right—but kine is Homer's word for cattle, which is apropos here.

only the French do. Therefore, King Charles's head has come to mean any great obsession. (Mr. Dick in *David Copperfield* was always using the phrase, you may remember.) Watergate has recently been the King Charles's head of American politics, as Communism was during the McCarthy era. You can try a more personal note, however: "Leonard nags so much about my spending money, it's become the King Charles's head of our marriage."

☞ **Canossa.** Remember this one? It was the castle in northern Italy where in the eleventh-century Holy Roman Emperor Henry IV went to Pope Gregory VII as a penitent, and the Pope kept Henry waiting in the snow for four days. So, "to go to Canossa" means to humble oneself, but good. "Simpson sure blew the Kleenex account, but if I know that old buzzard he'd rather lose his neck than go to Canossa."

☞ **Rubicon.** That's the river in Italy Julius Caesar crossed when the Senate had ordered him to stay put. Hence, "crossing the Rubicon" means committing yourself irrevocably to some course of action. "When Grace decided to have that affair with George, she not only crossed her Rubicon, she drowned in it."

☞ **Philippic.** Not just a big speech but a tirade— the kind of invective Demosthenes heaped on King Philip of Macedon, father of Alexander the Great. So: "Helen, please don't bore us with a big Philippic. Just say you hate his guts, okay?"

☞ **Philippi.** Recall your high school Shakespeare and you'll remember this is the place where Mark Antony defeated Brutus and Cassius. Now it's any place or situation where a final showdown occurs. Club tennis finals coming up? When you see your opponent the evening before, sing out a cheery "We'll meet at Philippi." Of course, he may look puzzled and reply,

"Philippi? But it's here, at ten o'clock." Just make sure some other members hear that little exchange.

☞ **Pyrrhic victory.** Pyrrhus was King of Epirus, in ancient Greece, whose military victories over Macedonia and Rome were so costly he might just as well have lost. Hence, any victory achieved at immense cost. "Doris may win all the arguments, but her victories are Pyrrhic—Frank's going to leave her one of these days." Or, "Oh, Les was brilliant, all right. He really made the chairman look like a fool—a Pyrrhic victory if ever I saw one."

☞ **Hobson's choice.** A seventeenth-century English stable owner named Thomas Hobson became famous—why? one wonders—for giving his rental customers only one choice, the horse nearest the stable door. Thus, the "choice": you take what's offered or you take nothing at all. E.g., "I know Max is not the greatest catch in the world, but at my age, dear, it's Hobson's choice."

☞ **Coventry.** To send someone to Coventry is to refuse to associate with him, to ostracize him. It has something to do with the English city, but nobody knows quite what. "After the way Simpson behaved himself last Saturday night, I'm afraid the membership will send him to Coventry for sure."

☞ **Sword of Damocles.** Greek legend once more. Damocles was a flattering courtier of Dionysius, King of Syracuse and a tyrant of the first order. Damocles had been carrying on about how the gods smiled upon his sovereign, who then invited him to a banquet and seated him beneath a sword suspended from the ceiling by a single thread—thus demonstrating, with sardonic whim, the precarious nature of the happiness of kings. Thenceforth it has symbolized imminent disaster:

"Since Grace found out I wasn't in Pittsburgh Tuesday night, I've been living under the sword of Damocles."

☞ **Bed of Procrustes, or Procrustean bed.** Those Greeks again! Procrustes was a nasty soul, a thief by profession, who owned an iron bed on which he compelled his victims to lie. He then stretched or cut off their legs so they would fit the length of the bed. Theseus finally got rid of the fellow, but the torturer's couch has left behind a term for inflexibility, the tendency to find conforming solutions that are arbitrary and often imposed. Try this out at a dinner party: "Every city has its own special problems in urban renewal, and I say the Administration's bill is Procrustean."

Faced with blank stares, gaping jaws? Go ahead and explain it to them. Politely . . . but slowly. You might as well enjoy every minute of it. Of course your superior knowledge may very well infuriate them. In that case just say you're willing to be sent to Coventry but you're damned if you'll go to Canossa.

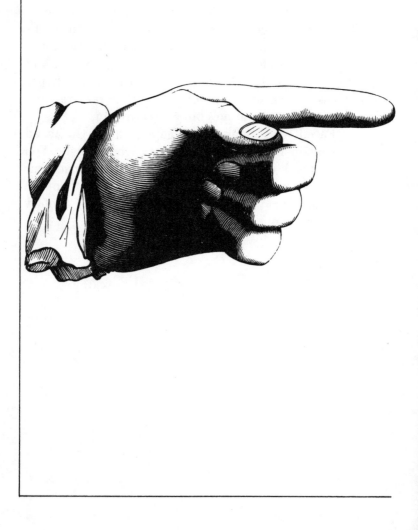

16
PATOIS ON THE POTOMAC

No social or business gathering of more than twenty minutes' duration fails to turn its hypercritical attention to Washington. What are the nation's duly elected representatives—those scoundrels—up to now?

Such conversations are dominated by insomniacs. How else explain all that information they suck in from newspapers, news weeklies, books, and editorial opinion from the *National Review* to the *New Republic?* The other type of tyrant is the highly opinionated. Whether conservative, liberal, or radical, one who comments on every event from a base of passion easily grabs the forum from those to whom the news is simply the news, who believe that there is some truth in the middle.

There is only one way for those more balanced in their views and too busy with important reading matter like the sports pages or Doonesbury to counteract the truly informed and the dogmatic. The secret? Give the impression that you are the insider, while they are mere observers. The technique should be familiar by now—use the trade talk of the Capitol, in an offhand manner. Imply that you hang your coat in the cloakrooms on the Hill.

Notice that one says "the Hill"—not Congress or Capitol Hill. Nor do you, unlike the uninitiated layman, use "lobbyists"; rather, speak of grantsmen or facilitators. If a bill is under consideration on the Hill —say, one Senator Jacob Javits is sponsoring—you remark, "I've been in touch with a facilitator who's close to Jack Javits' AA." That doesn't mean the senator has joined Alcoholics Anonymous; it refers to his administrative assistant. Staff people are always key figures in any legislator's office, and referring to the man *behind* The Man shows that you know where it happens.

"I have word that the Ledbetter Tidelands bill is ready for markup this week." Such a sentence sets you apart from the herd. Markup is what a committee or its staff does to the bill originally introduced. While your audience is still wondering what markup means, you zap them: "I figure it'll be the fifteenth before we have a *clean* bill." That's the way the back-room boys say that all changes, editings, and compromises have finally been incorporated.

As for having a bill ready for the fifteenth, Washington has its own way of dealing with time. If you ask, thinking you're savvy, "When will H.R. 1276 be reported out of committee?" you're out of it. The proper query is, "What's the *time frame?*"

Nor do you say, "I think they'll get to the measure the week of July 15." In Washington, "there's a *window* in the week of July 15" (through which, presumably, the work can squeeze through).

At a time certain is another favorite idiom of the District and, if it sounds like legalese, you're right. It means "at a specific time."

When arguing for a bill or administrative action, Washingtonians don't merely say there's a *need* for it. Rather, it is a *perceived need.* The academic advisory community in Washington—humanitarians all—talk instead about a *felt need.*

When a bill is finally okayed by the President, Federalese for the event is *signed off on.*

Washington abounds in such special language. The nice, simple word "money," for example, has given way to *funding.* So much more businesslike, so much less crass. Projects are never financed; they are *funded.* Maybe it's easier for congressmen to allocate funds than to just plain spend the taxpayers' money.

The Washington-hip do not cancel, kill, or even terminate a project; that is far too direct. Instead, you are *"phasing out* in that area." Why? Murmur, *"Counterproductive."*

You can transfer such tripe into other spheres obviously, for the effect of the unexpected: "I find most of Milton's marketing suggestions counterproductive." Or —borrowing another bureaucratic phrase—at your next PTA meeting try characterizing a rival proposal as *constructively negative.* Or, if you've been given the job of putting on a presentation for the Garden Club, or running a panel discussion for a Rotary lunch, borrow a term much favored in the Pentagon. Such an event is referred to as a *dog and pony show.*

The Washington crowd was the first to be enamored of *parameters.* Webster assigns several meanings to the word, but the Potomac crowd use it as synonymous with boundaries, limits, or criteria. Thus: "Unless the U.S.-Tibetan birth control assistance program is funded with at least eighty million, we'll never operate within congressional parameters."

Washingtonians also have a strange but definite aversion to the word "about." They won't say, "I'd like to talk about the foreign aid budget for Upper Silesia." They'd much rather talk *in relation to, with regard to,* or *with respect to.* For a change of pace they might talk *in terms of.* Even their wives echo this peculiarity. At the ragged end of one Georgetown dinner party we heard a woman say to her spouse, "George, I believe we should think in terms of going home."

Jargoneers in one field are sponges for the jargon of another. So it's not surprising the bureaucrats find computerese compelling. They don't work with someone any more, they *interface* with him, in order to benefit from his *inputs.* And they sincerely hope that their actions won't produce an avalanche of *negative feedback.*

Watergate added a lingo of its own, a final crime against the country. One writer described it as "a blend of men's locker room, corporate slang, and pop psych." The language was enriched (or polluted, depending on your politics or aesthetics) by such items as *stone-*

walling (a flat refusal to cooperate); *stroking* (manipulating people, as in the axiom, "Different strokes for different folks"); and *going the hangout road* or *modified limited hangout* (to tell the truth, or a selected part of it). "Hangout" apparently originated with the black phrase, "Let it all hang out." *At this point in time,* which means "now," was much ridiculed when the first Senate Watergate hearings were televised, but it gained a foothold in the language.

Military language is a separate division of Potomac patois, with so many entries that the Army has had to include a buzz-word glossary in its latest edition of the Staff Officer's Handbook. But with this book, not theirs, you can hold your own. Always refer to the Department of Defense as DOD, the Pentagon as *the puzzle palace,* a combat officer as a *muddy boots type,* and an error as a *glitch.*

One other characteristic must be noted. Washington would still be a swamp today without all of its many agencies and their alphabet soup abbreviations. Residents toss the initials around like Frisbees. There are more than a hundred by now, which is confusing and boring and you could easily mix them up. Remember the following half dozen: HUD (Housing and Urban Development), HEW (Health, Education and Welfare), FEO (Federal Energy Office), OMB (Office of Management and Budget), NSC (National Security Council), and EPA (Environmental Protection Agency).

Finally, you should know that firing people in Washington is *de-hiring,* or even fancier. The higher you go the fancier the language gets. Our friend George, for example, had a good job at HEW but was *unilaterally abrogated.* Was he downcast? Certainly not! Career bureaucrats don't die or fade away, they just move to another agency. When I asked George what he would do next, his calm reply was pure Federalese: "I am," he said, "re-examining my options."

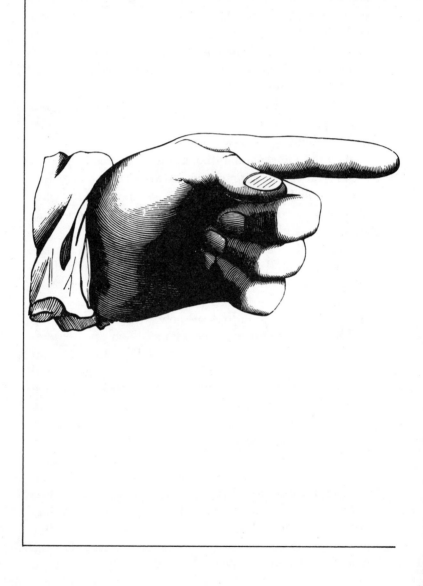

17
AND NOW
FOR A BREEZY
REDUCTIO
AD ABSURDUM

And there you have it, folks: a multidisciplinary macrosystem *pour le sport* of verbal jousting. Though this gallimaufry has a certain Toynbee-esque universality, it contains no crypto-strategies, no Delphic dicta; it is open, simple, a fully integrated game plan, straightforward as a Fibonacci sequence. By using the various subsystems you will always have contingent reserves with which to leverage your own storage bank of truth and trivia. Not since the Code of Hammurabi have directives for human behavior been more lucidly inscribed.

Of course you must not display your full panoply of cognitive powers all at once, as we do in this heuristic and admittedly pleonastic epilogue. One needs the subtlety of Sinon to establish the vincibility of one's fellows—not to mention the playfulness of a Firbank to savor it. (Ronald, of course.) Though we believe this quasi-chrestomathy fills a felt need, we do not claim it is *Weltbewegend!* Some would say it is not even an inclusive *catalogue raisonné*.

No matter. It is enough to know that next time you meet a curmudgeonly churl bloated with *amour-propre* you can approach him confidently, feeling, as Tennyson said, that your "strength is as the strength of ten."

But that was not the purposive thrust of this paradidactic hornbook. Rather, like Boniface among the Frisians, we sought to offer assurance, encouragement to the benighted. And now, with a *sang* markedly more *froid* than when you began, you can achieve dominance among peer-positioned conversationalists. Thus programmed, you can become, *tout à coup*, a lingual arriviste.

Viel Glück. Vsego horósega. Udacha. Bonne chance.

好 彩

Or, to be utterly derrière-garde about it—good luck!